Mel's
A-Cookin'

with a *d-d*-dash
of *h-h-h*-humor!

D1301070

Mel Tillis

This book was set in Times by Vanatech Systems, Inc.
The editor and book designer was Susan Klopfer.

Mel's A-Cookin' *(with a dash of humor)*

ISBN 0-9651629-8-2
Published by Spellbound Ink, a division of
Pegasus Creations

About Mel ...

Country music legend LONNIE MELVIN TILLIS grew up in Pahokee, Florida, a little farming community on the south eastern shores of Lake Okeechobee. After graduating from Pahokee High School, Mel attended the University of Florida.

He served in the U.S. Air Force from 1951 to 1955, moving to Nashville, Tennessee in 1957. Mel has written over 1,000 songs; over 600 songs have been recorded by major artists including "Detroit City," "Ruby, Don't Take Your Love To Town," "Emotions," "Snakes Crawl At Night, " I Ain't Never," "I'm Tired," "Burning Memories," and "Thoughts of a Fool."

As a recording artist, Mel recently completed his 60th album. He's had nine number 1 singles and 34 Top Ten singles. Mel has been in 14 major movies including "Smokey And The Bandit," and has appeared on dozens of talk shows including Johnny Carson, David Letterman, and TNN-Nashville Now

His major awards include six years as Music City News Comedian of the Year, 1976 Country Music Association Entertainer of the Year, Nashville Songwriters Hall of Fame Inductee, 1992 BMA Entertainer of the Year, 1993 BMA Songwriter of the Year, Great Empire Broadcasting, Inc. Album of the Year, and 1993 Country American Magazine, Branson Show of The Year.

In 1996, Mel was inducted into the Branson Hall of Fame, and voted Male Entertainer and Male Vocalist of the Year by the Branson All American Entertainment Awards. Tillis has built a new 2,700 seat theater in Branson, Missouri where he performs two shows six days a week.

Dedicated to Mama and Daddy

Contents

Introduction

Dear Chefs,

    I have been asked to write the introduction to my friend
Mel's cookbook. I don't know if this is good or bad! I do know
Mel is a great cook. If you're looking for fantastic recipes, this
is the book. The only problem I see is if you're trying to lose
weight — chew the cover. When we filmed "Uphill All The
Way," I weighed 150 pounds. When we finished the picture I
weighed 250 pounds! Mel cooked for me almost every day. He
said he was trying to make me jolly. Mel cooked the entire cast
Thanksgiving dinner, so I know he's a great cook.

    You won't be disappointed in this book — Happy Eating!

Roy Clark

Mel and Roy on the set of "Uphill All The Way."

Mel's A-Cookin'

Cowboy Mel

Gettin' Started

I *got started cookin' or tryin' to cook when I was 9 years old. I remember very well the first time I tried — I got a whuppin' for it, too. (The kind you don't forget.)*

We lived in Plant City, Florida in an old unpainted house on South Cherry Street. Our daddy was workin' as a chef on a dredge boat in Puerto Rico, while mama worked closer to home at the cannin' plant.

The year was 1941 and WWII was raging in Europe. 'Bout everything was rationed in those days: food, gas, tires, nylon hose. You name it.

There were three of us siblings at the time. My sister, Imogene, was the eldest. She's five years older than I, and Richard, my brother, is 13 months my senior. My younger sister, Linda, didn't come along 'til 11 years later.

Although we lived in south Plant City, we bussed to school out in the county, six miles from home in what was called Turkey Creek. It was a regular nine months school, exceptin' it started in April and let out in December, just before Christmas.

We were out January, February, and March so the school boys and girls could pick strawberries during berry season. We were paid 2 cents a quart, and if you were a real fast picker and didn't goof off, you could make a dollar or two in a day's work. And that was good money in those trying times.

The berry money went a long way in helping to buy our school clothes, a few groceries. With a leftover quarter every Saturday, we could go to the picture show and see Gene Autrey and still have enough left over for candy, popcorn, and an RC Cola.

The bleeding hearts of today would say that was child labor, and should be considered cruel and inhumane. I heartily disagree with that kind of thinkin'. It taught me the value of the all mighty dollar; it taught me how to respect other folk and their property, made me a Republican for life, and taught me how to cook.

We attended school all through the long summer days, and usually got home 'bout four in the afternoon. On one of those afternoons, and like most kids when they get in from school, I was starvin' and I wanted somethin' to eat. And I wanted it bad.

Now, mama always warned us when she left for work not to play with matches or light the kerosene stove or by tryin to cook 'til she got home. She said she was afraid we'd set the house afire. And I almost did. Here's how.

I decided on fried potatoes. I'd watched her slice 'em up like potato chips and fry 'em up good and brown in a cast iron skillet filled with grease maybe a thousand times. I peeled the skin off about six large spuds and sliced 'em up just the way she did it. I salt and peppered 'em real good.

Next, I turned the wick up a little bit more than mama

would have — I wanted me a good hot fire for them taters. I struck one of those big old strike 'em anywhere matches and lighted the wick. It flared up there right nicely, so I put the skillet on the stove and spooned 'bout 3 pounds of lard into it. Mama later said that was enough grease to cook 50 pounds of potatoes, and I guess it was.

Now I prided myself in knowin' that I was suppose to let the grease get hot before I put the potatoes into the skillet to cook. I ate two or three raw ones, waiting for the grease to get hot enough.

The grease was smokin' pretty good when I dumped those wet Idaho spuds into the skillet. Well, sir, that hot grease bubbled over the sides of the pan onto the wick below and fire shot up almost to the ceiling of that old house. Scared me to death. This was not how mama did it.

There was a washtub settin' on a stool in the middle of the kitchen that mama would use to soak our dirty overalls in. I snatched that burnin' inferno off the stove and hurled it into the tub of dirty clothes.

And let me tell you, no one could have made a bigger mess if they'd tried. There was Octagon soap suds, grease, overalls, dirty water, and sliced potatoes all over everything.

Mama said she'd never seen "such a mess in all her born days." I stuttered I was "so-so-orry", and that I'd "never do that again."

But being sorry wasn't enough. After we walked two miles there and back to the doctor's office (I'd burned the fingers on my left hand pretty good), she put a whuppin' on me (the liberals would have called it child abuse), that I shall never forget. And brother I needed it, too.

Speakin' of whuppin's, don't get me wrong here. I'm not talkin' 'bout some of those plow line whuppin's like you see in the movies. I am talkin' 'bout mama's switchin's, the kind that made you jump and holler like you was just 'bout to die. I got so many such switchin's as a boy, my buttocks and legs thought they were natural resources.

I guess, seein' that she couldn't keep on whuppin' us (Richard and me) forever, (I can't recall Imogene ever gettin' one) and that we were intent on learnin' to cook, she began showin' us how to make certain things. She let us lick the spoons when she'd make certain things like muffins, cakes or cookies, and she'd let us take turns churnin' for butter.

We'd sing a little song that mama taught us. It went like this:

"Come butter come, come butter come. Johnny's at the garden gate waiting for his butter cake. Come butter come, come butter come."

It worked, too. Mama sometimes let us collect the butter and put it in the molds. Boy! We felt like that we were really doin' something'. And we were. You could look and see what you'd done.

We'd watch her cut up okra to fry and sometimes she'd stick the tops of the okra pods on our foreheads like they were horns. We'd get down on our hands and knees and crawl about

12

the kitchen mooing like we were cows. That would really tickled her funny bone.

Mama taught us how to fry cabbage and she'd give us the stalks to eat. There is nothing better than a raw cabbage stalk 'less maybe it is a broccoli stalk. You can fry 'em, too. Most people don't know that.

We learned to cook all kinds of greens: polk, turnip, mustard, spinach, and collards. I guess I like collards the best; I'll tell you how I cook them, later on.

Big lima beans are easy to cook. I still cook a pot of beans or field peas once a week. Mama always served them over rice and I do the same. I keep a 25 pound bag of rice in my pantry at all times.

We learned how to make corn bread from scratch. Nowadays, all you have to do is add buttermilk and egg to self-rising meal, mix it altogether, and bake it in the oven or fry it in a skillet on top of the stove. Either way works well.

Mama showed us how to take a coke bottle and pound red meat to make it more tender. She had all kinds of ways of doin' things to save money when it came to preparing a meal. She had to, and we never missed a meal.

Daddy, when he was home, had a hand in teachin' us, too. He cooked somewhat different than mama. For instance, if it called for a pinch of somethin', he'd put two pinches. "More is always better," was his motto. He and mama couldn't get along in the kitchen at all. Mama said he was wasteful. Daddy said she was stingy.

I guess that is where I get my singular way of thinkin' when it comes to cookin' or bakin'. My wife and I surely don't see eye to eye when it comes to whippin' up a dish. She has her own way of doin' things and I have mine: The way mama and daddy taught me.

I suppose I've said enough 'bout gettin' started, haven't I? So without further adieu, as the old preacher use to say, "I'm gonna get right into the message."

On the following pages of this recipe book, you're going to find recipes from about every state of the Union. I've been in every one of 'em and have collected these recipes wherever and whenever I could.

Some of these recipes are mine. Some are things I've concocted by experimentin' with other folks concoctions. Some are mama's and some are daddy's and some of these recipes are from friends of mine from my days in Pahokee, Florida. . . folks like Babs and Marie UpTheGrove, Aunt Eula Tillis, Alice Spooner, J.C. (James) Sims, and Frank O'Connell, to mention a few.

All of mama's sisters (there were eight) were good cooks, and Aunt Vergie could really make the best cakes.

You'll find snapshots of my family, along with many other pictures taken over the last eighty years, as well as anecdotes and stories that I tell on stage from time to time.

I hope you enjoy this effort and will write me and let me know how you are doing with the recipes. Thank you for invitin' me into your kitchen. God Bless You and happy cookin'.

Mel

SECTION I

Mel's Favorite ... Appetizers

Richard, 6; Imogene, 10; and Mel, 5

WELCOME TO THE SHOW!

I'd like to welcome all of you to the show. My name's Mel Tillis and I'm Pam's daddy. We've got a great show lined up for you tonight; my only problem is that I've only got two hours to do it all in. And you know, in Vegas, if you go over your allotted time, they say it cost 'em fifty thousand dollars a minute. If this is true, then one night in 1981 at the Frontier Hotel, I cost 'em over six hundred and eighty seven thousand dollars, and f-f-f-fifty two cents!

I did folks, I t-t-t-tried to do the auctioneer. Heyyy! Don't laugh. I sold three goats and a bulldog.

If I have any creditors here tonight, don't worry, don't worry. I've been a-practicin'. That's right, I've been a-practicin'. I've had me some th-th-therapy, too. And it ain't wo-wo-workin'.

Mel Tillis, on stage

APPETIZERS

♦ Cheese Ball
♦ Anchovy Biscuits
♦ Buffalo Chicken Wings
♦ Shrimp Magdalene
♦ Broccoli Dip
♦ Guacamole
♦ Stuffed Mushrooms
♦ Mel's Stuffed Jalapeno
♦ Pahokee Meat Balls
♦ Mexican Cheese Dip

Party Cheese Ball

1/2 cup chopped walnuts
3 to 5 ounces blue roquefort cheese
8 ounces package cream cheese
1/4 teaspoon garlic salt
1 tablespoon chopped green pepper
1 tablespoon chopped pimento
2 tablespoons chopped stuffed olives may be substituted
 for the pepper and pimento

Heat oven to 350 degrees. Spread walnuts in a shallow pan
and toast, stirring occasionally, until golden brown (8 to 10
minutes). Blend cheeses; stir in the garlic salt, pimento and
green pepper. Chill until firm, then shape into a ball and roll in
toasted nuts.

Serve with any kind of cracker you want.

Anchovy Biscuits

1 3 ounce package of soft cream cheese
1 stick of butter
1 cup of flour
Anchovy paste or filets

Mix cream cheese, butter and flour together. Store in the refrigerator until well chilled. Roll the dough paper thin, then cut out in round pieces and fill each with small pieces of anchovy paste or filets. Fold and seal tightly and bake at 450 degrees for about 5 minutes.

You can make these ahead of time, stored and unbaked in the freezer.

Buffalo Chicken Wings

25-30 Chicken wings
Vegetable Oil
1/3 cup margarine
1/2 to 3/4 bottle of Louisiana Hot Sauce, according to taste.

Soak wings in salted ice water, using 1 cup of salt for approximately 1 hour. Deep fry 'bout half the wings at a time, in hot oil until they are nice and brown, probably 'bout ten minutes. Depends on you and the amount of heat you got going. Just keep your eye on them and you'll be all right.

Next, drain the wings well. Melt margarine in large wok or saucepan. Add 'bout 1/2 bottle of hot sauce; stir until well blended. Now, some folks like their wings real hot, like 'em good people down 'round Pearl River, Louisiana. *If you like 'em like dat, put de hole damn bottle in.*

As for our brothers to the north, if you like 'em milder, like I do, just add more margarine. Next, put them chicken wings in a large metal bowl and pour the margarine hot sauce mixture over the wings; mix well. *They are ready to serve!*

Shrimp Magdalene

2 dozen large shrimp (mighty expensive these days)
3 tablespoons green onions, chopped
1 tablespoon green bell pepper, chopped
1 tablespoon red bell pepper, chopped
1 tablespoon yellow bell pepper, chopped
2 tablespoons celery, chopped
1 stick of butter
Salt
White pepper or black
1/2 pound fresh mushrooms
2 tablespoons parsley, snipped
4 tablespoons lemon juice
2 teaspoons Worcestershire sauce

Peel and clean uncooked shrimp, leaving the tails on. Saute onions, peppers and celery in butter for 4 or 5 minutes. Add shrimp. Sprinkle with salt and pepper, cook and stir until the shrimp are nice and pink.

Add mushrooms and cook for 1 minute. Do not overcook. Add parsley, lemon juice, and Worcestershire sauce. Mix well. Serves 6 to 8 as an appetizer, if shrimp are large enough.

Words of wisdom. He who sitteth upon a hot stove will surely riseth again.

Broccoli Dip

2 packages frozen chopped broccoli
1 small onion, chopped
2-3 stalks of celery, chopped
1 6 ounce roll of garlic cheese
1 can cream of mushroom soup
1 4 ounce can of mushrooms, drained
3/4 cup slivered almonds
1 small can of water chestnuts, quartered
Pimiento for color
1/2 teaspoon salt
1/4 teaspoon pepper
2 tablespoons butter
1 teaspoon monosodium (Don't ask me to pronounce this ingredient) glutamate
1 teaspoon Worcestershire sauce
1/4 teaspoon tabasco sauce

Cook broccoli the way they tell you to on the package; in other words follow their directions. Let it cool in a strainer and drain at the same time. Combine all ingredients. Warm thoroughly and serve in a chafing dish.

Guacamole

2 Florida avocados, mashed
1 tablespoon lemon juice
2 tablespoons lime juice
1 tablespoon onion, grated

1 teaspoon salt
1/4 teaspoon chili powder
Pinch of cayenne pepper
1/3 cup salad dressin' or mayonnaise. I prefer salad
dressin'. It's a matter of one's taste.
1/4 cup ripe olives, chopped
4 slices of crisp bacon. (I use the microwave for crispier
bacon.)

Blend all above ingredients thoroughly.
Serve with warm corn chips, ribs of celery or spoon over
lettuce as a salad.

Stuffed Mushrooms

3 pounds medium sized mushrooms
2 jars Smithfield ham spread

Remove stems from mushrooms. Clean caps with a damp
cloth; do not rinse in water. Fill with ham spread, place under
broiler in the oven and broil for 3 minutes. *Serves quite a few
folks.*

Stuffed Jalapeno

2 dozen jalapeno peppers
1 package cream cheese
12 strips of bacon, cut in half, leaving you with 24 half
strips of bacon.

Wash peppers thoroughly, then cut the top and stem off
each one. With a small pointed knife remove seeds and any
pithiness you might find in the jalapeno. Hold under faucet
and make sure all the seeds have floated out.

Fill jalapeno with cream cheese and wrap each one with bacon strip. Insert a wooden toothpick through the bacon and the jalapeno holdin' it together while bakin'. Bake in oven at 350 degrees until bacon gets brown.

Do not overcook. Keep your eye on 'em.

Pahokee Meat Balls

1 pound ground beef
1 small onion, finely chopped
1/2 teaspoon horseradish
Salt and pepper to taste
1 1/2 slices of bread, broken
1/2 cup of milk
1 cup catsup
2 tablespoons Worcestershire sauce
1/2 cup fruit syrup from pineapple
1/2 cup water
4 8 ounce cans of button mushrooms
3 6 ounce cans pitted black olives, or large green olives not stuffed.

Combine ground beef, onion, horseradish, salt, pepper, bread and milk and mix 'em all together then shape into meat-balls. Bake in the oven at 350 degrees or fry in a skillet until done, not overcooked.

In a metal mixin' bowl combine catsup, Worcestershire sauce, fruit syrup, and water. Arrange meat balls in a chafing dish with mushrooms and olives. Pour sauce over all and heat. *Yummy, yummy, they're good!*

Mexican Cheese Dip

4 tablespoons margarine, melted
4 tablespoons flour
1 heaping teaspoon dry mustard
1 teaspoon chili powder
1 teaspoon cumin
1 teaspoon pepper
1 tablespoon catsup
2 cups milk
Jalapeno pepper, crushed
8 ounces American cheese
1 garlic clove, chopped

On low heat stir margarine and flour together. Remove from heat and add mustard, chili powder, cumin, pepper, and catsup. Return to heat and then add milk, jalapeno pepper, cheese and garlic. Cook over low heat until thick.

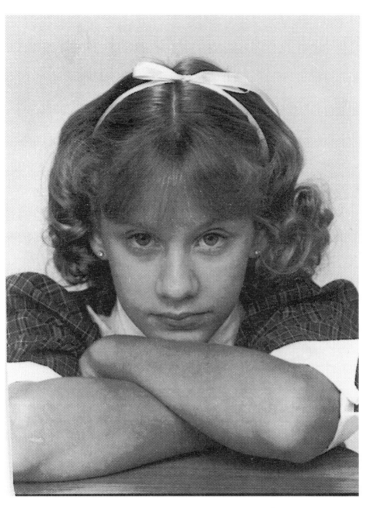

"What's dad cookin' up this time?" (Carrie April)

SECTION II

Mel's Favorite ... Beverages

Mel and his family on stage

DOCTOR ZELLER

I'm talkin' pretty good these days. My only problem is, I can't remember nothing. My wife noticed it, too, but she notices everything. She thinks she's Mary Tyler Moore.

She called my doctor and said, "Doctor Zeller, I'm so worried 'bout my husband. I think his mind is a-wanderin' on 'em."

He said, "Mrs. Tillis, I know your husband, and don't you worry. He won't get far."

HAD ME A BIRTHDAY

Had me a birthday not too long ago. I woke up one mornin' and I was a senior citizen; you heard me right, I didn't stutter — a senior citizen. And hey, my plans are made. I'm gettin' me an RV camper and a poodle dog, and we're goin' to Branson. I'll see you there.

My wife is always gettin' me things for my birthday that I can't use. August the eighth, 'bout four years ago, she got me a m-m-m-mule, that's right a m-m-mule, a metal mule. He's out there in front of the theater. Did y'all see 'em out there? Well, that's my birthday, and I want all of you to know that you are welcome to have your picture made with my m-m-m-m-, with my m-m-m-m-, jackass, if you like.

First time I seen that old mule they blindfolded me, yeah they blindfolded me. Somebody spun me 'round several times, made me dizzier than an outhouse rat, then they led me outside and spun me again.

Somebody said, "look up." Well, I looked up but I couldn't see nothin'. Finally, after a lot of gigglin' and picture takin', they removed the blindfold. And I said, "The last time I seen a jackass that big, we elected him." That can be anybody you want it to be, you know. After all, it's your vote.

BEVERAGES

♦ Daddy's Egg Nog
♦ Mint Julep
♦ Cuban Coffee
♦ Hot Spiced Tea
♦ Fruit Slush Punch
♦ Pink Punch
♦ Orange Frost
♦ Southern Iced Tea
♦ Lemonade-Cranberry Punch
♦ Orange Flip

Daddy's Egg Nog

6 eggs, separated
3/4 cup sugar
2 cups milk, chilled
1 to 1-1/2 cups Cognac or brandy
1/4 cup rum
2 cups heavy cream, chilled
Nutmeg (optional)

Beat egg whites until almost stiff enough to hold a peak. Add sugar gradually, beating until stiff but not dry. Set aside.

Beat egg yolks until thick; stir in milk, Cognac and rum, blending well.

Whip cream until stiff and fold into egg-milk mixture. Fold in beaten egg whites. Keep cold until ready to serve. Pour into punch bowl and sprinkle with nutmeg, if desired. Makes about 3 quarts.

Wonderful to serve around Thanksgiving and Christmas holidays.

Mint Julep

1 teaspoon sugar
1 tablespoon water
12 sprigs mint
4 ounces brandy
Fresh pineapple or other fruit
Rum to taste

In an old fashion glass, dissolve sugar with water and add 6 sprigs of mint. Muddle and pack with crushed ice. Stir and add brandy. Decorate with a piece of pineapple or other fresh fruit and remaining mint leaves. Add rum. Place in freezer for about ½ hour to frost glass. Yields 1 drink.

Cuban Coffee

Nutmeg
1 scant teaspoon brown sugar
3/4 ounce brandy
3/4 ounce triple sec
3/4 ounce Tia Maria
6 ounces hot coffee
Whipping Cream, whipped

Dampen rim of an 8 ounce stemmed glass and dit it into a mixture of nutmeg and brown sugar. In glass pour brandy, triple sec, Tia Maria and fill with coffee. Top with whipped cream. Yields 1 drink.

Hot Spiced Tea

1-1/4 cup sugar or equivalent of sugar substitute
3 teaspoons whole cloves

3 teaspoons whole allspice
4 sticks cinnamon
1 cup red hot cinnamon drops
Juice of 12 lemons or 2 cans lemon juice concentrate
9 cups boiling water
6-8 tea bags

Put sugar, spices, red hots, and lemon juice in boiling water. Let boil until cinnamon drops dissolve and until mixture is spicy enough. In separate pot, make 2 quarts medium strength tea, using tea bags. Strain spicy mixture and add to tea. Pour into containers and refrigerate. Heat as wanted. Keeps indefinitely. Makes 4 quarts.

Fruit Punch Slush

2 cups sugar
4 cups water
20 ounces pineapple juice
3 mashed bananas (blender or potato masher)
1 (12 ounce) can frozen lemonade
1 (12 ounce) can frozen orange juice
4 quarts 7-Up
2 teaspoons lemon juice

Boil sugar in water until dissolved. Cool and add the next four ingredients. Mix well and freeze in two containers. Thaw 2 hours before using. In punch bowl pour 7-Up and lemon juice over frozen mixture to serve.

Pink Punch

1 package frozen strawberries

1 large can pineapple
1 package frozen raspberries
1 bottle claret or rose'
1 package frozen peaches
2 cups gin
1 cup sugar
1 large bottle of ginger ale
1 cup rum
Lemon or orange slices

Combine first five ingredients and let stand overnight. Squeeze through cheesecloth. Add remaining ingredients. Makes 6 quart.

Orange Frost

1-1/2 cups evaporated milk diluted with 1½ cups
        water
1-1/2 tablespoons sugar
½ cup chipped ice
1-1/2 cups orange juice
2 teaspoons grated or finely chopped orange rind

Put diluted evaporated milk and sugar into fruit jar or shaker. Shake well with chipped ice. Add orange juice and rind and shake vigorously.
Serves 6.

Southern Iced Tea

Make double strength hot tea, allowing 2 teaspoons tea for each cup boiling water. Pour hot over crushed ice in tall glasses. Sweeten to taste.

Lemonade Cranberry Punch

4 pints cranberry cocktail
4 6 ounce cans frozen concentrate for lemonade.
11 teaspoons allspice
1/2 teaspoon salt
4 cups water

Combine ingredients in large kettle; heat and simmer gently 10 to 15 minutes.
Do not boil. Pour into punch bowl and serve in mugs. Makes about a gallon punch.

Orange Flip

1 egg beaten until fluffy
Juice of 2 large oranges

Have both egg and orange juice cold. Combine and beat together just enough to blend, about 2 seconds. Serve immediately. Serves 1.

Words of Wisdom: Where the hen scratches, there layeth the worm.

Mel enjoys a relaxing moment.

SECTION III

Mel's Favorite ... Soups

Mel and his son, Mel, Jr. ("Sonny Boy")

THE LOVEBOAT

*L*ast August my wife took me on the Loveboat for my birthday. Yeah! On the Loveboat. Went all down 'round in the Bahama Islands on the Loveboat.
I remember one day we were all out on the deck gettin' some sun. I was all laid back in a contour chair, with the contour mattress and the contour pillow. Hey man! I was contoured out.
My wife said, "I'm thirsty, honey. I'm goin' for some ice tea. Would you like for me to bring you somethin', my sweetness?" That's the way they talk on the Loveboat. But the minute it touches the dock, that's all over with, bud.
Anyway, I said, "Yes my dear. You can bring me some decaf coffee, with a little cream and a little sugar. You'd better write it down my darlin', you know how forgetful that you are."
She told me to shut my mouth. Right there in the Bahama Islands on the Loveboat. On my birthday. 'Bout 15 minutes later here she comes back and says, "Here's your eggs, honey, just the way you wanted 'em. Over easy."
I said, "I told you to write it down. I wanted 'em scrambled."
I can't have nothin'.

SOUPS

- ♦ Cream of Corn Soup
- ♦ Rice Soup
- ♦ Seafood Chowder
- ♦ Cracker Fish Chowder
- ♦ Corn Chowder
- ♦ Chicken Gumbo
- ♦ Florida Avocado Soup
- ♦ Imogene's Bone Soup
- ♦ Okeechobee Oyster Gumbo
- ♦ Clam Chowder

Cream of Corn Soup

16 ounces finely chopped corn (or can of corn)
2 cups boiling water
1 sliced onion
2 cups milk

Add boiling water to corn and cook 20 minutes. Scald onion in milk, remove onion and add the milk to the corn. Mix:

1 teaspoon sugar
1/8 teaspoon black pepper
2 tablespoons flour
2 tablespoons butter, melted
1 teaspoon salt
Whipped cream for decoration

Add enough of liquid from corn to make the consistency to pour. Then combine mixtures, stir and heat. Put 1 tablespoon of whipped cream in each bouillon cup, pour in hot soup *and pass the salted popcorn.*

35

Rice Soup

1 3 pound hen
8 cups water
1 onion, chopped
1-1/2 cup chopped ham
Pimiento, chopped
1 clove garlic
1/2 teaspoon ground oregano
2 tablespoons vinegar
2 tablespoons salt
1/2 teaspoon pepper
1 tablespoon capers
1/2 cup tomato sauce
1/2 cup olives, chopped
1 pound rice
1 cup peas (English)
1 cup Parmesan cheese
6 Pimiento strips

Cut up chicken, boil in 8 cups water until about half done, reserving 6 cups of broth. Saute onions and ham, add chopped pimiento, chopped garlic, oregano, vinegar, salt, pepper, capers, tomato sauce and olives. Mix chicken well in to this mixture. Then add rice and 6 cups broth to chicken and above seasoning. Cook over slow fire until rice is tender, add peas. *This makes a thick soup. To each serving add a strip of pimiento and sprinkle with cheese.*

Seafood Chowder

1 small fresh lobster tail
1 pound fresh shrimp
5 cups boiling water

1 small onion
2 teaspoons salt
1 bay leaf
2 thick slices lemon
1 pound sea scallops

Put lobster and shrimp in boiling water with next 5 ingredients and simmer for 15 minutes. Remove seafood from the stock. Cool. Shell shrimp and remove vein. If large, split lengthwise. Remove meat from lobster tail shell. Cut into easy to eat size pieces. Return shrimp shells and lobster shells to the stock and simmer together 30 minutes.

Strain stock. Add to stock sea scallops cut into quarters (or 1 pound tiny pearl scallops, uncut; these latter have the more delicate flavor, but are not easily come by). Add:

1 pound filet of sole or halibut
2 cups diced potatoes

Cook for 15 minutes. Remove the filets, flake the fish coarsely and remove any bones that are left. Return to the stock containing the scallops and potatoes.

1 6-1/2 ounce can crab meat
2 medium onions, chopped
1/4 pound bacon, diced

Remove the bits of shell from the can of crab meat, and add the crab meat to the stock. In the bottom of a 6 quart soup kettle add onions and saute until golden with diced bacon. Stir in:

1 tablespoon curry powder
1 teaspoon salt
1 quart of fish stock

2 cups cream
3 cups milk

Add the lobster meat and shrimp to the other cooked fish, vegetables and stock. Season with:

1 teaspoon paprika
1/8 teaspoon pepper
Dash of Tabasco

Add 2 tablespoons butter or margarine and heat together until almost boiling. It should never be allowed to boil. Taste for seasoning and fix it up, if needed, to suit your own taste. Serve in chowder bowls with cress or parsley chopped as fine as possible. Serves 8 generously.

More of one or the other kind of fish may be used - if one fish must be omitted (two lobster tails for one lobster, for instance). Or you could skip the crab meat and add more scallops.

Cracker Fish Chowder

2 tablespoons bacon, chopped
1/2 cup onions, chopped
1 cup potatoes, diced
2 cups hot water
1 pound fish filets
1 cup milk
1 cup cream
1 teaspoon salt
Dash of pepper
Dash of paprika

Fry bacon crisp. Add onions and brown lightly. Add potatoes and water. Cook until potatoes are almost done. Cut fish and cook until it flakes when tested with a fork. Add milk and cream with seasonings. Do not boil after milk is added. Serve hot. Serves 6.

Corn Chowder

3 slices bacon
1 large onion, chopped
2 cups diced, pared potatoes
2 cups water
8 ears corn, cut and scraped off cob
1 cup milk
1 cup light cream
1-1/2 teaspoon salt
1/4 teaspoon pepper
2 tablespoons butter

Fry bacon in deep pot. Remove bacon. Cook the onion in bacon drippings until yellow. Add potatoes and water. Cover and cook 20 minutes. Add corn, milk, cream, salt and pepper. Cover and simmer slowly 15 minutes.

Just before serving add butter and crumble bacon over chowder. Serve hot. Makes 6 to 8 servings.

Words of Wisdom:
When in doubt, turn right.

Chicken Gumbo

1 fryer, cooked
1/4 pound bacon, diced
1/4 cup onion, chopped
1/4 cup green pepper, diced
1 cup celery

3 sprigs parsley, finely chopped
1 cup tomatoes, fresh or canned
4 cups chicken stock
Salt and pepper
1/2 teaspoon thyme
2 cups okra, sliced
1 cup cooked rice

Debone chicken and cut into medium sized chunks. Saute bacon in soup pot. Add onion, green pepper, celery and saute. Add parley, tomatoes, stock and seasonings. Slowly simmer until vegetables are soft. Add chicken, okra and rice; cook for 10 more minutes. Serves 6.

Florida Avocado Soup

1 large avocado
1 cup chicken broth
1 cup whipping cream
2 teaspoons lemon juice
Salt and pepper to taste
Red Caviar

Peel avocado and blend. Mix with broth. Stir over low heat until smooth. Add cream, lemon juice, sale and pepper. Stir well, cool. Chill in refrigerator. Serve sprinkled with caviar. May substitute fresh dill or julienned cucumber for caviar. Serves 4.

Imogene's Bone Soup

3 pounds lean, boneless stew meat, cut in small pieces

1 medium soup bone
1 tablespoon salt
2 (1 pound) cans tomatoes
1 large onion, chopped
5 ribs celery, chopped finely
1/4 small head cabbage
2 large carrots, sliced finely
Black pepper to taste
1 teaspoon thyme
3 bay leaves
Dash cayenne
1/4 pound spaghetti
Green beans, drained and chopped
3/4 cup okra, fresh
1 large white potato, cubed

Into a large, heavy stewing pot place a gallon of cold water, stew meat and soup bone. Add salt. Boil, skimming frequently until contents are clear, about 1 hour. Continue a gentle boil and add tomatoes, onion, celery, cabbage, carrots and seasonings.

Cover and gently boil until vegetables and meat are tender. Add remaining ingredients and cook until potatoes are tender. You may need to add more water as soup is cooking. Serves 6 to 8.

Okeechobee Oyster Gumbo

1-1/2 tablespoons minced onion
4 tablespoons butter or margarine
1 pint oysters
4 cups fish stock or canned clam broth
1 cup cooked or canned okra
2 cups cooked or canned tomatoes
Salt and pepper
2 tablespoons flour

Cook onion in 2 tablespoons butter until lightly browned. Add oysters and their liquid, stock, okra, tomatoes, and sale and pepper to taste. Bring slowly to boiling point. Add a smooth paste made of 2 tablespoons of butter and flour. Stir until smooth. Serves 4 to 6.

Clam Chowder

6 slices bacon
1/8 teaspoon white pepper
1/2 cup of water
1/3 cup onions, chopped
1 cup potatoes, diced
1/4 teaspoon salt
1-1/2 cups of milk
1-1/2 cups evaporated milk
1 (7-1/2 ounce) can of clams
Parsley

Chop bacon, fry until crisp. Remove bacon from skillet. Drain on paper towel. Add pepper, water, onion, potatoes and salt to grease in skillet.

Cook for 10 minutes then add both milks and claims. Cook 10 more minutes or until potatoes are tender. Add bacon and sprinkle with parsley. Serve hot. Serves 4.

SECTION IV

Mel's Favorite ... Salads

Mel's a'fishin'!

I'M GONNA HAVE A BABY

I got up early this mornin', five o'clock, 'cause I wanted to beat the traffic to Wal-Mart. I needed to go to Wally World, they got everything, you know. If they ain't got it, you don't need it.

Well sir, I got on 76 Country Music Boulevard and it took me an hour and a half to go a mile and a half on the boulevard. There was a lady in back of me in her car and she kept a-honkin' her horn at me. Oh…she honked, and she honked, and she honked, and she honked. Finally, I had enough of her honkin' and I stuck my head out the window and said,

"Lady, will you please quit honkin' your horn at me. I can't do nothin' 'bout all of this."

Well, she stuck her old head out the window and said,

"I've got to get out of the traffic, sir. I'm goin' to have a baby."

I said, "Lady, you ought not to have got in the traffic in that condition."

And she said, "I didn't."

LITTLE DUCK

Here's a funny story my little girl brought in from school one day. Her name's Hannah. She's nine years old, and she sings in the show.

It's 'bout a duck, a little duck. And it went into the grocery store one day asked the manager,

"Do you have any duck food?" And the manager said,

"No, we don't have any duck food, and besides that, we don't allow little ducks in here, now get out." Well, it left and it came back the next day and asked the manager,

44

"Do you have any duck food?" And the manager said,

"No, I told you that we didn't have any duck food and if you come back in here again, I'm gonna get some nails and nail your little webbed feet to the floor. Now get out." So it left, and it came back the next day, and asked the manager,

"Do you have any nails?"

The manager, furious, said

"No, we don't have any nails!" And the little duck said,

"Well, do you have any duck food?"

SALADS

♦ Potato Salad
♦ Imogene's Fruit Salad
♦ Mexican Rice Salad
♦ Cranberry Salad
♦ Cole Slaw
♦ Shrimp Salad
♦ Marinated Slaw
♦ Caesar Salad
♦ Heart of Palm
♦ Seven Layer Salad

Potato Salad

10 medium sized potatoes
5 hard-boiled eggs, diced
1 cup sweet pickle relish
1 large onion, chopped
1 teaspoon salt
1/2 teaspoon pepper
1-1/2 cups salad dressing
1 teaspoon vinegar
1/2 teaspoon mustard
1/2 teaspoon sugar

Boil potatoes with jackets on until tender. Let cool; peel and cube. Add eggs, pickle relish, onion, salt and pepper. Mix lightly. In a separate bowl, combine salad dressing, vinegar, mustard and sugar. Mix well; add to potato mixture and stir together, being careful not to mash potatoes. Refrigerate. *This is better if made several hours ahead or overnight before serving.* Serves 10-12.

Imogene's Fruit Salad

12 oranges (sectioned)
1 (#303) can pears, chopped
1 (#303) can crushed pineapple
1 small jar maraschino cherries, drained
2 large red delicious apples, peeled & chopped
4 bananas, sliced
1 cup chopped pecans
1/2 cup sugar (optional)

Section oranges, removing seeds and squeeze remaining juice from oranges into bowl; add chopped pears and juice, crushed pineapple, whole cherries, peeled chopped apples, sliced bananas and chopped pecans. Add sugar to taste. Chill and serve.

Delicious. This recipe has been in my family for as long as I can remember. It can be used as a fruit cup or served with pound cake as a dessert.

Mexican Rice Salad

1/2 pound rice
2 tablespoons oil (cooking)
1 large onion, chopped
4 large ripe tomatoes, mashed
3 red chile peppers, mashed
4 cups soup stock
1/2 teaspoon salt

Wash rice and drain. In the oil, brown rice partially,

add onion until slightly brown, add tomatoes, chile peppers, salt and boiling soup stock to rice and onions. Cook slowly until rice is done.

Cranberry Salad

1 cup sugar
1 package cherry jello
1 package ground cranberries
1 cup hot water
1 cup strained crushed pineapple (reserve juice from
    pineapple)
1 cup orange pulp
1/2 cup pecan nut meats, chopped

Combine 1 cup sugar with 1 package cherry jello into a dish and pour 1 cup hot water into this to dissolve. Then add the strained crushed pineapple, orange pulp, ground cranberries, nut meats, and 3/4 cup juice that was left from the strained pineapple. Place in the icebox to congeal and stir frequently until well blended.

Cole Slaw

1-1/2 cups shredded carrots
1 head cabbage (about 4 cups)
1/2 teaspoon salt
2 teaspoons sugar
1 tablespoon vinegar
3 tablespoons mayonnaise

Combine carrots, cabbage, salt, sugar and vinegar. Moisten with mayonnaise. Mix lightly. Arrange on crisp lettuce or in large salad bowl. Sprinkle with minced parsley or paprika. Serves 6.

Shrimp Salad

2 cups cooked shrimp, chopped
Salt
1 cup celery, diced
Pepper
1 teaspoon lemon juice
Mayonnaise

Mix lightly all ingredients except mayonnaise and refrigerate. Just before serving, drain and toss with enough mayonnaise to hold ingredients together. Serve on crisp lettuce. Garnish with tomato and lemon wedges, hard-cooked eggs or ripe olives. Serves 4.

Marinated Slaw

1 head cabbage, finely shredded
1 green pepper, cut into strips
1 large onion, sliced into rings
1/2-3/4 cup sugar
3/4 cup oil
2 teaspoons dry mustard
2 teaspoons celery, chopped
1 cup vinegar
2 teaspoons salt

Combine cabbage, green pepper and onion rings. Pour sugar over this. Combine last five ingredients in a saucepan. Bring to a boil. Combine the two mixes and marinate for 24 hours stirring occasionally.

Caesar Salad

2 heads romaine lettuce
2 heads iceberg lettuce
2 bunches scallions, chopped
1 pound bacon, fried and crumbled
1 box garlic croutons, or homemade croutons
Parmesan cheese, grated

Make salad and toss in bacon, adding croutons last. Add dressing and sprinkle salad with cheese.

Dressing

1 cup Wesson Oil
1 teaspoon minced garlic
1 egg
1 teaspoon salt
1 teaspoon sugar
Juice of lemon

Make dressing blending all ingredients well. A large wooden bowl is the best in mixing a Caesar salad. Refrigerate at least one hour. Some people also will add anchovy to this recipe; this is optional.

Heart of Palm and Artichoke Hearts

1 can hearts of palm, drained and diced
6 pimiento strips
1 can artichokes, drained and sliced

Place diced hearts of palm and sliced artichoke hearts

on lettuce leaf; garnish with pimiento strips. Pour dressing over salad. Serves 6.

Dressing

1 cup salad oil
1/4 teaspoon dry mustard
1/3 cup vinegar
1/4 teaspoon cayenne pepper
1 teaspoon lemon juice
1 teaspoon sugar
1/2 teaspoon salt
1 clove garlic, mashed
1/2 teaspoon celery salt
Dash of paprika

Combine all ingredients in a jar; cover and shake. Makes about 1-1/2 cups.

Seven Layer Salad

1 head lettuce
1 diced red onion
1 package frozen peas
1 can water chestnuts, sliced
1-1/2 cup mayonnaise
1 tablespoon sugar
1 package grated cheese
3 hard boiled eggs

Layer deep salad bowl with lettuce, onion, frozen peas, sliced water chestnuts, mayonnaise, sugar and grated cheese. Sprinkle boiled eggs on top. *This salad is best after one day in refrigerator.* Serves 6-8.

SECTION V

Mel's Favorite ... Breads

Mel and grandson, Marshall, in a scene from "Big River"

A 20-year-old Mel, in the U.S. Air Force

IN THE AIR FORCE

I used to be in the Air Force and I was stationed on Okinawa; it's a part of the Ryukyu's Islands in the South China Sea. I was a baker — that was my job. I didn't wanna' be a baker. I wanted to be a pilot. I wanted to fly one of them fighter planes, but they told me "No way, Jose!"

The way I talked, I'd never get the clearance to land one of them airplanes; I'd run out of gas, for sure.

And they were right. Can you imagine me havin' to bail out in a parachute at 10,000 feet? By the time I got to t-t-t-two, it would be curtains for me. But, I served my country; I served 'em cakes, cookies, pies, and donuts.

One year, I believe it was in 1952, it was 'bout three weeks b'fore Christmas and I wanted to get my mama something different for her Christmas present.

I went down to one of the little villages outside the air base and shopped around all mornin'. I shopped and I shopped. I noticed every other little shop had birds for sale, all kinds of birds.

The Japanese people are crazy 'bout birds. So, I bought mama a bird. Aww....., it was a pretty thing. They said it was exotic; had all the colors of the rainbow. He was 'bout the size of a bantam rooster, and mama loved bantams. Always had several runnin' round in the yard.

I shipped the bird home to Florida and on Christmas Day, I tried to place a long distance call in to her, but the lines were all tied up by others tryin' to call their parents or loved ones.

'Bout midnight on Christmas Day, I finally got one of the operators on the line; I tried with all my might to tell her what number I was tryin' to reach.

Tired of waitin', she hung up on me. 'Bout three days went by b'fore I got that call through. Christmas had already come and gone.

I said, "Mama! How'd you like the bird?" And she said,

"Well son, he was a little gamey."

I cried, "Mama! You cooked the bird? Mama, he was an exotic bird. He could talk better than I could t-t-t-talk."

And she answered, "Well, that bird ought'a said something, son."

WORKED FOR THE RAILROAD

After I served my country for four years, I was honorably discharged in December of 1955. I went home to Florida and looked 'round for me a job. Daddy said it was time to go to work.

Well, I found jobs but I couldn't hold 'em. My cousin, James, got me a job where he worked. I was for the Atlantic Coast Line Railroad. I hired on as a fireman. One of my duties as a fireman was to call out the signals to the engineers as we approached 'em while runnin' the locomotive on the mainline, a very, very important responsibility.

For instance, a green light is the signal for All Clear; yellow or amber is the signal for Caution; and a red light is the signal for Stop. Those signals were always two or three miles behind us b'fore I could say, "R-e-e-e-e-ed."

I lost that job. Well, I didn't exactly lose it; I was fired.

HARRY COOKIE TRUCK

Next, my brother, Richard, got me a job driving a "Harry's Cookie Truck" as a cookie salesman. My route was in Belle Glade and Pahokee, Florida. And I said,

"Hey! Piece of cake! I know everybody in both those

towns, I'll make a killin'."

I drove for old Harry for three weeks and I didn't sell one cookie, not one! And you know somethin'?

I don't blame 'em people. I wouldn't eat a Harry cookie, either.

DETROIT CITY

I didn't give up; a friend of mine said come up to Detroit, and he's get me a job at one of the automobile factories. So I went to Detroit and I got me a job, working on an assembly line. My job was to count the cars as they went by. Sixty cars went by 'fore I could say, "There goes the f-f-f-first one!"

Seeing as how that wasn't gonna work out, they put me to workin' on the shock absorber line. The told me where to stick 'em. And I told 'em, well, I lost that job, and that was when I went to Nashville and became a songwriter.

Thank God I didn't have to talk to do that.

2602 MORGAN STREET

Folks are always askin' me, "Mel Tillis, where are you from?"

Well, I'm from Tampa, Florida originally born in an old house on 2602 Morgan Street. Almost in Ybor City. (That is the Cuban section of Tampa.) My daddy worked at Henderson's Bakery, there.

It was in that old house on Morgan Street that I got bit by a mosquito, which gave me an eight month battle with malaria. I won that battle, but after that I started stutterin', which today, I suppose, is my trademark.

I told somebody the other day, "You know, I been talkin' so good here lately, I'm gonna have to go back down to Morgan Street and get bit again."

BREADS

♦ Muck Steppers Hush Puppies
♦ Daddy's Hot Rolls
♦ Mel's Hot Water Cakes
♦ Mayonnaise Biscuits
♦ Mama's Buttermilk Biscuits
♦ Mexican Corn Bread
♦ Hatton's Fritters
♦ Tater Bread
♦ Herb Rolls
♦ Broccoli Corn Bread

Muck-Steppers Hush Puppies

1-3/4 cups water-ground corn meal
4 tablespoons flour
1-1/2 teaspoons salt
3 teaspoons baking powder
1/4 teaspoon pepper
1-3/4 cups milk
2 eggs, slightly beaten
1 large onion, chopped fine

Mix corn meal, flour, salt, baking powder and pepper.
Add milk and eggs. Stir to blend. Add onion and blend.
Water or more milk or corn meal may be added to produce
desired consistency.

Drop spoonfuls of batter into hot fat or shape into
small patties and place flat. Dropped hush puppies are lighter
than hand shaped ones. Fry until lightly browned on one side,

turn and brown on the other side. Drain on absorbent paper.
Makes 6 servings.

There's a band of top soil that stretches 20 miles or so around the southeastern shores of Lake Okeechobee. In some place this top soil is 20 feet deep. It is called "muck" — And if you lived there for any length of time, you were called a "muck-stepper."

Daddy's Hot Rolls

1 package yeast
1/4 cup warm water
4 tablespoons shortening
3/4 cup milk
4 tablespoons sugar
1 teaspoon salt
1 beaten egg
3 cups flour, sifted

Dissolve yeast in warm water. Melt shortening then add milk, sugar, salt, egg and yeast in the order named. Stir the sifted flour into this mixture. Cover and let rise until double in a warm place.

Work out on a well floured board and roll out 1/4 to 1/2 inches thick. Cut with biscuit cutter and brush with melted butter. Make a crease just off center with back of knife. Fold over and crease edges. Brush with butter, let rise again and bake in hot oven 400 degrees until brown.

Mel's Hot Water Cakes

1 cup corn meal
1/2 teaspoon salt
1 cup boiling water
2 teaspoons melted far or butter

Sift the corn meal and salt through a coarse sifter into a bowl. Add the boiling water and stir to form a stiff dough. Dip hands into cold water. Then mold dough into flat oval cakes about 1/2 to 3/4 inch thick.

Drop into hot oil and fry until crisp. When done, these hot water cakes will be crusty on outside and moist inside. Break into pieces and serve hot with butter. Makes 4 servings.

Words of wisdom: If you're left handed, when in doubt, turn left.

Mayonnaise Biscuits

2 cups self-rising flour
4 tablespoons mayonnaise
1 cup milk

Combine all ingredients. Drop in to greased muffin tins. Bake at 450 degrees until done. *Easy, easy!*

Mama's Buttermilk Biscuits

1 package yeast
1/2 cup warm water
5 cups all purpose flour
1 tablespoon baking powder (fresh)
1 teaspoon soda
1 teaspoon salt
3 tablespoons sugar
3/4 cup Crisco - or lard
2 cups buttermilk (Mama would sometimes use
   clabber milk.)

Dissolve yeast in warm water. Sift dry ingredients and cut in shortening until mixed thoroughly. Add buttermilk and dissolved yeast. Mix well. Roll on floured board and cut as for biscuits. Bake at 400 degrees for about 12 minutes. Makes 6 dozen. You may cook small amount and store unused dough in refrigerated in a covered bowl. Will keep two weeks or more.

Mexican Corn Bread

1 cup corn meal
1/4 cup oil
1 cup buttermilk
2 jalapeno peppers, chopped
1/2 teaspoon salt
3/4 teaspoon soda
1 8-ounce can cream style corn
2 eggs

Small onion chopped
1/4 pound mild Cheddar cheese, grated

Combine all ingredients, except cheese. Heat oil in a
heavy skillet. Pour half of batter. Sprinkle half of cheese over
batter. Pour remaining batter and top with remaining cheese.
Bat at 400 degrees for 30 minutes.

Hatton's Corn Fritters

3 eggs, separated
6 ears fresh corn, cut and scraped off cob (or 1
    8-ounce can cream-style corn)
1 scant cup flour
1 teaspoon salt
1 teaspoon paprika
1 tablespoon sugar
2 teaspoons baking powder

Beat egg yolks. Add corn, flour and seasonings. Fold
in stiffly beaten egg whites, add baking powder. Drop by
tablespoon into hot grease. Serves 6.

Those Hattons were the best sweet corn growers in
the world. When I was in the Air Force on Okinawa, we'd get
crates of fresh sweet corn with the Hatton Brothers label on
it. I'd tell all the boys, "That's where I'm from, Pahokee,
Florida."

Tater Bread

2 packages yeast
5-1/2 - 6 cups all-purpose, flour, sifted

1-1/2 cups milk
2 tablespoons butter
2 tablespoons sugar
2 teaspoons salt
1 can cream of potato soup

Combine yeast and 2-1/2 cups flour. Heat milk, butter, sugar and salt until warm. Add to dry ingredients in mixing bowl. Add potato soup. Beat at low speed for 1/2 minute, scraping sides of bowl. Beat at 3 minutes at high speed. Stir in by hand enough of remaining flour to make a moderately stiff dough. Turn out onto lightly floured board. Knead until smooth, 5-8 minutes. Place in a greased bowl, turning once. Cover; let rise until in double in size, 50-60 minutes. Punch down. Cover; let sit 10 minutes.

Divide dough in half; shape into two loaves. Place in 2 greased 8-1/2 x 4-1/2 inch loaf pans. Let rise until double in size, about 25 minutes. Bake at 400 degrees for 25-30 minutes.

Herb Rolls

1/2 cup butter (not oleo)
1-1/2 teaspoons parsley flakes
1/2 teaspoon dill weed
1 tablespoon onion flakes
2 tablespoons Parmesan cheese
1 (10 or 11 ounce) can refrigerator buttermilk biscuits

Melt butter in 9 inch pan. Mix hers and cheese together and stir into butter. Let stand 15-30 minutes. Cut biscuits into halves or fourths and swish around in herb-butter to coat all sides. Bake at 425 degrees for 12-15 minutes. This may be prepared several hours ahead and refrigerated.

Broccoli Corn Bread

5 eggs, beaten
1 large onion, chopped
10 ounce package frozen chopped broccoli,
     thawed and drained
1-1/2 sticks melted butter
2 cups cottage cheese
2 tablespoons sugar
2-7 ounce packages Jiffy corn bread mix

Mix all ingredients and put into greased 9" x 12" pan or 11" iron skillet. Bake 1 hr., or until good and brown on top, at 350 degrees. The broccoli can be substituted with cauliflower also.

I never cared too much for broccoli until I tried this recipe. It was given to me by a girl who works for us at the theater. Her name is Cookie, and you'll love the recipe.

The Sparrow Sails Again

by Cindy Westmoreland

The Sparrow, a Pacific Seacraft Flicka 20 ft. yawl, recently was willed to Mel by his late, great friend, Burl Ives. Ives, America's best loved folk singer, recently passed away after a long illness. Mel and Burl were very close and over the course of 35 some odd years developed a special bond. Mel and Ives sailed several times together in the Bahamas back in the 1960's and spent many hours writing calypso songs. Burl was an inspiration to Mel and touched his life forever. One of Burl's great passions was sailing.

After his death, *The Sparrow* was picked up in Washington state and made the long journey back to Missouri. *The Sparrow* has been refurbished with the help of David Payne, our chief maintenance man. Once completed, Mel and his son, Mel, Jr., took up sailing and *The Sparrow* sails once again on Table Rock Lake.

Mel commented that Burl would sit proudly at the helm, look around, and utter one word while sailing ..."Nice!"... in a manner that only Ives was known for. Was Burl trying to teach Mel something by leaving him *The Sparrow*? Undoubtedly, as Mel finds sailing very peaceful. Thank you Burl for bringing us *The Sparrow*. She sails once again!

SECTION VI

Mel's Favorite ... Seafood

The Sparrow sails again

THORNDYKE TILLIS

In 1939 we moved to Pahokee, Florida. Pahokee is a little farmin' community on the banks of Okeechobee Lake. And that's where I grew up, and where I call my hometown. I got a lot of friends, and I still got some kinfolks who live there. Got an old cousin down there, his name is Thorndyke Tillis. Named him after the general. I never could say that in them days, so I just called him T.T. Now, I could say that. One Sunday mornin' Brother Speares asked T.T. to stand and give us the Lord's Prayer. Well, he was sort'a slow in standin' and ol' R.D. Hickman hit me with his elbow and said, "I bet you a quarter he don't know it."

And I said, "I ain't got a quarter."

And he said, "Nickel."

And I said, "Nickel."

Ol' T.T. stood up and said, "Now I lay me down to sleep, I pray the Lord my soul to keep."

R.D. said, "Here's your nickel, I didn't think he knew it."

A BITCH TO IRON

Folks are always askin' me 'bout the family. Hey! I got a house full of young 'uns. I got me five girls and one boy, which proves that stutterin' ain't got nothin' to do with it.

My oldest is Pam. We're awfully proud of Pam; her records are goin' gold and platinum these days, and her videos are great, too. I've got a story 'bout Pam when she was just 4 years old, and even at that age she could sing, and well, too. We'd take her to church on Sunday, as we always did, and one Sunday our pastor asked to her to get up b'fore the congregation and sing without accompaniment, and she did.

She was well received by the congregation and after she'd finished her son, the preacher came down from the altar and congratulated her.

And she said, "Thank you, sir."

Then he asked her, "How long have you been singing, Pam?"

And she replied, "All my life, sir."

"That's wonderful," he said. "And that is a beautiful, beautiful dress that you are wearing."

And she said, "Thank you, sir, but my mama said it was a bitch to iron!"

SEAFOOD

- ♦ Mel's Very Best Seafood Gumbo
- ♦ Dad's Okeechobee Catfish Filets
- ♦ Baked King Mackerel
- ♦ Shrimp Scampi
- ♦ Fried Mullet
- ♦ Baked Mullet with Spanish Rice
- ♦ Shrimp Creole
- ♦ Barbecued Shrimp
- ♦ Baked Fish in Sour Cream
- ♦ Baked Whole Sea Trout

Seafood Gumbo

7 tablespoons flour
6 tablespoons oil
4 ribs of celery, chopped

2 medium onions, chopped
1 medium green pepper, chopped
1 clove garlic, chopped
2 cans of stewed tomatoes
2 14-1/2 ounce cans tomato sauce
2 quarts water
6 crabs, cleaned
3 teaspoons salt
2 Bay leaves
Red pepper, to taste
2 tsp. Parsley flakes
1 large package frozen chopped okra
3 pounds peeled, deveined shrimp
1 pound crab meat
1 pint oysters

In a heavy bottomed 4 quart pot, make a dark roux of flour and oil, stirring constantly so as not to burn. When brown, add celery, onions, green pepper and garlic. Stir this with roux until vegetables become slightly browned.

Add stewed tomatoes and tomato sauce. Bring mixture to a boil, stirring frequently. Add crab bodies (excellent for flavor) and seasonings and boil gently for 1 hour. Taste for additional seasonings and add okra and cook for another hour.

Add peeled, raw shrimp, crab meat, and oysters. Cook for 30 minutes longer, tasting again for seasonings. The crab bodies may be removed before adding the seafood. Add more water if gumbo becomes too thick. Serve over rice with french bread and a green salad.

Dad's Okeechobee Catfish Filets

Catfish filets
White or plain yellow meal
Salt and pepper

Drop filets into a paper bag with enough white or yellow plain meal to suit you. Add salt and pepper to taste, and shake it all up 'til the filets are well coated with meal. Take one of those strik'em anywhere matches and drop it into the grease. When the match catches on fire, start droppin' in the filets. When the filets come up from the bottom and float, they're done, friends. You can let'em brown a little if you want to, but they're done.
This recipe can also be used for fried mullet or other fish.

Baked King Mackerel

1 large onion, chopped
2 ribs celery, chopped
2 tablespoons butter
2 cups packaged bread crumb dressing
Parsley
Lemon
Garlic salt
White wine
Salt
Pepper
1 large king mackerel filet

Saute chopped onion and celery in butter. Add bread crumb dressing and remaining seasonings. Mix well. Salt and pepper filets. Place one filet in a buttered baking dish and spread with dressing. Place other filet on top of dressing, creating a sandwich effect. Bake at 325 degrees until done. Baste with additional butter during baking.

Shrimp Scampi

1/2 to 1 cup olive oil
2 teaspoons salt
Pepper to flavor
4 cloves garlic, pressed
2 pounds raw, deveined, peeled medium-sized shrimp
1/2 cup Port wine
1 tablespoon lemon juice
2 tablespoons minced fresh or dried parsley

Place enough olive oil in heavy iron skillet so that the oil covers a depth of about 1/4 inch or more. Add salt, pepper and garlic. Cook over moderate heat until garlic is golden. Shrimp should be thoroughly dried before used. Shrimp should be slit down back so they will open fantail when cooked and juices can be absorbed, also known as "butterflying the shrimp." Add shrimp, wine and lemon juice. Cover and cook over low heat for 15 minutes. Shake pan from time to time and spoon some of the liquid over the shrimp. Just before shrimp are done, add parsley. Place shrimp in soup bowls and pour savory liquid over or serve over steamed rice. *Wonderful!*

Shrimp Creole

1 pound shrimp
3 tablespoons butter, melted
1 cup chopped onions
1 cup chopped green pepper
1 clove garlic, chopped
1/4 teaspoon paprika

1 can tomato sauce
Salt and pepper to taste

Peel shrimp; remove veins. Mix and stir in melted
butter, onion, green pepper and garlic. Let this simmer until
peppers are tender, then add tomato sauce, salt, pepper and
paprika and boil 5 minutes. Add raw shrimp to this and boil
not over 10 minutes.

Black Mullet with Spanish Rice

Flour
Salt and pepper
1 3-pound fresh water mullet or snapper
6 tablespoons melted butter
1/4 cup chopped onion
2 cups chopped celery
1/4 cup chopped green pepper
1 tablespoon Worcestershire sauce
1 tablespoon catsup
1/2 teaspoon chili powder
1/2 lemon, sliced thinly
1 bay leaf
1 minced garlic clove
1 teaspoon salt
2 teaspoons sugar
3 cups canned tomatoes
Dash cayenne pepper

Mix flour, salt and pepper and coat mullet inside and
out. Melt butter in skillet and over low heat, cook onion,
celery and green pepper for 15 minutes. Add all remaining
ingredients and simmer until celery is tender. Press mixture
through potato ricer; pour sauce over cleaned fish and bake in
350 degree oven 45 minutes, basting frequently with Spanish
sauce.
Serves 4.

Barbequed Shrimp

2 pounds raw shrimp, peeled and deveined
1/3 cup minced onion
3 tablespoons olive oil
1/2 cup hot water
2 teaspoons mustard
2 tablespoons Worcestershire sauce
1 cup catsup
1/4 teaspoon salt
1/3 cup lemon juice
1 teaspoon chili sauce
2 tablespoons brown sugar

In heavy pan saute onion in olive oil until transparent. Add all remaining ingredients except shrimp to onion in pan. Turn heat low; cover and simmer 10 minutes. Place shrimp in broiling platter; cover with sauce.

With shrimp 6 inches below broiler, broil about 6 minutes or until shrimp are cooked. Turn once. Serve hot with remaining sauce. Serves 4.

Baked Fish in Sour Cream

3 pounds frozen fish filets
1/2 teaspoon salt
1/8 teaspoon pepper
1-1/2 teaspoons Accent
Onion rings
1 cup thick sour cream

Thaw fish, place in buttered or oiled flat baking dish

or oven-glass dish. Sprinkle both side of filet with salt, pepper and Accent; let stand 10 minutes. Cover fish with onion rings (slice onions thin; separate into rings) pour or spoon sour cream over onions. Bake uncovered in moderate oven 350 degrees until fish flakes easily when tested with a fork, about 30 to 35 minutes.

Baste fish occasionally with the cream and if liquid evaporates too fast, or fish seems dry, add a tablespoon or two of hot water. Serve from baking dish, adding fresh garnish.

Baked Whole Sea Trout

1 whole 2 pound sea trout, dressed
Salt and pepper
Lemon juice (optional)
1 garlic clove
1/2 cup dry white wine
1 (1 pound) can whole peeled tomatoes

Dip fish in and out of water lightly seasoned with salt or lemon juice. Dry with paper towel. Rub fish inside and out with garlic and some of the wine and place in buttered baking dish. Mash tomatoes with a fork or your hands and spread over fish. Season with salt and pepper.

Cover baking dish with aluminum foil and bake in preheated 400 degree oven 10 minutes per inch of thickness, or until fish flakes easily when gently probed with tines of fork. Serve fish with sauce from pan.

Imogene

Linda

Mel

Richard

Daddy

Mamma

76

SECTION VII

Mel's Favorite ... Poultry

MOLASSES

Here's a story my daddy used to tell me when I was just a little feller. I told this in my Sunday School class and you can tell it in your class, too, when you get back home.

It's about a family of moles, and there were three of them moles; papa mole, mama mole, and baby mole. And they lived under the ground in the molehouse.

One day, they were all on a mole trip. They were on vacation, and headed for Branson. And they were all in a row, 'cause that's how they travel, them little moles do, 'cause they can't half see.

And like I said, they were burrowin' along, and ol' papa mole had forgot his contact lenses, and he ran 'em all into the foundation of a building.

Well, he stopped abruptly. And mama mole piles into the rear end of papa mole, and baby mole piles into the rear end of mama mole. Ol' papa mole sticks his head up out'a the ground to get his bearin's and as he looks 'round he realizes that he's ran 'em all into the foundation of a pancake house. Now, he didn't know for sure, 'cause he couldn't half see, but he sniffed it out. He went like this --- sniff, sniff, sniff, sniff, sniff, sniff, sniff, sniff, sniff, sniff, and he said,

"Smells like pancakes to me, mama."

Mama mole sticks her head up out'a the ground and she sniffs it out. She went like this:

---sniff, sniff, sniff, sniff, sniff, sniff, sniff, sniff, sniff, sniff, sniff, and she said:

"Oh, yes! And it smells like honey to me."

Baby mole sticks his head up out'a the ground, but he didn't sniff it out. And he said,

"Well, it smells like mole-asses to me."

I went to Sunday School and told this, and Daddy gave me a whipping.

78

'FORE I COULD WALK

These two little boys 'bout 5 years old were in kindergarten. One little boy says to the other, "I got to go in Monday and get the operation that little boys sometimes have when they're little."

The other little boy said, "Yeah, I had that done to me when I was 3 days old."

First little boy, "Did it hurt?"

Second little boy, "Hurt! It took me a year 'fore I could walk!"

POULTRY

- ♦ Chicken and Rice
- ♦ Glades Chicken Wiggle
- ♦ Barbequed Chicken
- ♦ Mel's Chicken and Rice Supreme
- ♦ Italian Chicken Breast
- ♦ Chicken Broccoli Casserole
- ♦ Oven Fried Chicken
- ♦ Chicken and Dumplings
- ♦ Sand Cut Fried Chicken
- ♦ Mexican Chicken

Chicken and Rice

2 chickens (2-1/2 to 3 pounds)
Garlic salt to taste
Lemon juice, to taste

1/3 cup oil
1 large onion, chopped fine
1 green pepper, chopped fine
1 can tomato sauce
5 cups cold water or soup stock
1/2 cup sauterne wine
2 pounds rice, washed
2 red peppers, chopped
1 can asparagus
1 can petit pois

Cut each chicken into 8 parts and season them with garlic salt and lemon juice for at least 2 hours before cooking. Heat the oil and brown the chicken and set them aside. In that same oil add the onion and green pepper. Let them cook until soft but not brown.

Add the tomato sauce and let it simmer for 5 minutes, then add chicken and let it simmer for 2 or 3 minutes before adding the cold water or soup stock with the wine included.

Cover it and let it boil before adding the rice. Let it cook at medium heat until the rice starts to grow, then put on low heat until it finishes cooking. Add some of the petit pois and red peppers; and mix it with the rice.

Before serving, adorn the rice with remaining red pepper, petit pois and asparagus. Serves 8 to 10 persons.

Glades Chicken Wiggle

1 hen, stewed and boned
Chicken gravy

1 cup cooked celery
1 package frozen peas, cooked
1 can mushrooms, drained
1 package spaghetti, cooked
Salt and pepper
Paprika

Retain broth from stewing chicken, then thicken chicken gravy, add celery, peas, mushrooms, salt and pepper to taste. Serve over cooked, drained spaghetti. Garnish with paprika.

Barbequed Chicken

Use young chicken not weighing over 2 or 2-1/2 pounds dressed. Quarter for broiling. Brush with melted butter and then place skin side down directly on broiler pan, not rack.

Place in oven 5 to 7 inches under heat. Watch carefully and turn when light brown. When both sides have browned lightly, begin spooning barbecue sauce over chicken and keep turning and basting sauce over chicken. When well browned reset oven to lower temperature (350 degrees) and cook until tender. Time will depend on size of chicken and temperature of oven. Will vary from 45 minutes to 1-1/2 hours. It is possible to brown on both sides and cook at 300 degrees from 1-1/2 hours to 2-1/2 hours, eliminate much of the watching.

Sauce for chicken:

1 teaspoon salt
1/2 teaspoon black pepper
1 tablespoon paprika
1 teaspoon prepared mustard

1 tablespoon sugar
1/3 cup water
1/3 cup vinegar (or lemon juice)
2 tablespoons Worcestershire sauce
1/3 cup catsup

Blend salt, pepper, paprika, mustard and sugar. Add water. Heat to boiling. Remove from heat. Add vinegar or lemon juice, Worcestershire sauce and catsup.

Mel's Chicken and Rice Supreme

1 (4 pound) chicken (whole)
1/4 red bell pepper, chopped into small cubes
1/4 yellow bell pepper, chopped into small cubes
1/4 green bell pepper, chopped into small cubes
1 carrot, chopped into small cubes
1 stalk celery, chopped into small cubes
1 large onion, chopped into small cubes
3 cloves garlic, minced
3 cups Jasmine Rice (purchase at Oriental markets)
1 teaspoon salt
1 teaspoon black pepper
5 cups water or chicken broth

Cut up chicken in desired pieces and remove excess fat and skin; leave just enough for flavor. Put cut up pieces into a medium size pot. Chop the following into small cubes: red, yellow and green peppers, carrots, celery and onion. Add minced garlic and combine in same pot. Put rice into pot. Salt and pepper to taste.

Mix all ingredients by hand until well distributed. Add

5 cups of water or chicken broth. (If you use the broth, don't use any salt, the broth is plenty salty..believe me!) Put the pot with all the ingredients on the stove and bring to a boil. After it comes to a boil put the lid on the pot and turn down to low heat. Let cook at low heat for approximately 1 hour. Serves about 6 people.

Serve with potato salad, cranberry sauce, corn bread, green beans, corn on the cob and iced tea. You can top this off with homemade apple pie!

Italian Chicken Breast

4 chicken breasts
1 cup flour
1 teaspoon salt
1/2 teaspoon pepper
1/4 teaspoon Italian Seasoning
1 egg
1 cup milk
1 stick butter (unsalted)
8 tablespoons mushrooms
3/4 cup white table wine
Garlic to taste
3 cups cooked spaghetti

Debone chicken breasts. Cut each breast into two pieces. Mix next four ingredients; shake in bag until well blended. Whip egg and add milk. Dip chicken breast in milk and egg mixture, then into seasoned flour. Deep fry at 375 degrees for ten minutes. (Fry only a few pieces at a time.)

While the chicken breasts are frying, melt butter; add mushrooms and saute. Add wine and stir gently. Season with garlic. Now add cooked spaghetti and allow to simmer til chicken is tender (about 15 minutes. Stir to avoid sticking. To serve, place chicken breasts on hot platter. Pour spaghetti and mushrooms over chicken breasts.

Serve with your favorite garlic bread or "Herbed Rolls" found under the "BREAD" section in this cookbook.

Chicken Broccoli Casserole

2 packages frozen broccoli spears
2 cups cooked chicken breasts, cut up
2 tablespoons lemon juice
1/4 teaspoon curry powder
1 cup sharp cheddar cheese
2 cans cream of chicken soup, undiluted
1 cup mayonnaise
Cracker crumbs

Cook broccoli and place in casserole; cover with chicken. Mix next 5 ingredients and pour over chicken. Top with cracker crumps. Bake at 350 degrees for 30-40 minutes.

Oven Fried Chicken

1 cup cornflake crumps
1/4 teaspoon red pepper
1 teaspoon paprika
1/2 teaspoon garlic powder
1/4 teaspoon ground thyme
6 skinned breast halves
1/4 cup buttermilk

Combine first five ingredients in plastic bag. Shake to mix well. Brush both sides of chicken with buttermilk. Place in bag of crumbs and shake to coat. Place chicken on broiler pan which has been prayed with vegetable spray. Bake at 400 degrees for 45 minutes or until done. Serves 6.

Chicken and Dumplings

Stew chicken, when tender pick the meat from the bones and put in a large pot with tight fitting lid and add 4 cups of broth. Bring to a boil.

Dumplings:
1-1/2 cups flour
3 teaspoons baking powder
3/4 teaspoon salt
1-1/2 tablespoons shortening
3/4 cup skim milk

Sift together the dry ingredients and cut in the shortening. Stir in enough milk, mixing only to moisten the dough thoroughly. Drop by teaspoons into boiling chicken broth. Dip the spoon into the boiling liquid first so that the dough will slide off easily. Cover pan tightly and cook 15 minutes. Enough for 6 servings.

Sand Cut Fried Chicken and Gravy

Salt and pepper, to taste
1 hen, cut up
1/2 cup flour
1 small onion, chopped
Fresh minced garlic or dash of garlic salt
1-1/2 cups water

Salt and pepper chicken, roll in flour once piece at a time. Brown in a small amount of fat; remove from pan, use fat to brown about ½ cup flour, add chopped onion, a dash of garlic or minced fresh garlic. Add 1-1/2 cup water, salt and pepper to taste. Strain gravy, pour over chicken and bake in 325 degree oven for about 45 minutes. Serve with rice.

Mexican Fried Chicken

2 pounds chicken, boned
1 can cream of chicken soup, undiluted
1 onion, chopped
1/2 pound grated American
1 5-3/4 ounce bag nacho cheese chips, crushed
1/2 can Rotel tomatoes
1 can cream of mushroom soup, undiluted

Layer all ingredients in greased 9 x 13 casserole dish , beginning at top of list. Bake uncovered at 350 degrees for 30 minutes.

SECTION VIII

Mel's Favorite ... Beef

Carrie April

MISS ARMSTRONG

Speakin' of whuppins', and all, I remember one night I came in from church. It was on a Wednesday night, and I was 11 years old at the time. I wasn't too tall at 11 for some reason or another, but like I said, it was on a Wednesday night.

Daddy made us go to church every time the door opened. Now, that was all right with us, tho. We enjoyed ourselves, but he stayed at home.

Anyway, when I came home that night I had me two black eyes. And daddy said, "Son, w-w-w-w-, son, w-w-w-, son w-w-w-w-w-?

Daddy couldn't say nothin, either. And I sure wasn't gonna say anything 'til he got something said.

Finally, he got it out. And he said, "Son, where did you get the black eyes?"

And I said, "Daddy, I was in church, and I was being good."

It was hot that night folks, and I do mean hot. It was in the year of 1943, A.D., in the dog days of August, 'fore air conditioning. Everybody had one of them little funeral home fans they gave the churches back in them days. Everybody was just a-gettin' it with them fans. Looked like a bunch of bees, fannin' their hive to keep it cool.

Well, sir, all the congregation was perspiring p-p-p-rofusely, except for the lady in front of me. Her name was Miss Armstrong. Now Miss Armstrong was a large lady, a very healthy lady, sort'a fat complected. And she wasn't perspiring, brother, she was sweating.

Brother Moberg had been preachin' for an hour and a half, on a Wednesday night. Now, he didn't need to be preachin' that long, especially on my part, 'cause he had already saved me a week ago on a Wednesday night.

Finally, he asked us all to stand and sing from the hymnal, "His Eye Is On The Sparrow." Well, when Miss Armstrong stood up, I forgot all 'bout that sparrow. And like I said, I wasn't too tall at 11 --I just could see over those high-back pews they had back in them days.

But, I could see well enough to know that Miss Armstrong was a-sweatin' so bad that her dress was a-clingin' to her. Ya'll seen that 'fore I know; if you ain't, you ain't been nowhere, and I know you didn't come in here on a bus. And hey! It had gathered an bunched, too.

Well sir, I knew that lady had a problem. I knew it right then and there, cause her problem was a-starin' me right in my face.

All the folks in my pew, and all the folks in the pews in back of me were just a-laughin', and a-gigglin', and a-whisperin', and a-pointin'. I felt so sorry for Miss Armstrong, I truly did. I wanted to tell her, but I couldn't talk. I wanted to just reach out, and o-o-o-ow, I didn't know what to do. I just had been saved.

Well, I pondered her problem; I didn't know what else to do. Aw-----, I pondered, and I pondered, and I prayed 'bout it, too. And you know, I thought the Lord told me, but I found out it wasn't the Lord. It was R.D. Hickman. I thought it was the Lord, though, and I thought He said, "Melvin, here's your chance to do a good deed, and I'll write it down in the big tally book."

Well, when I got the word, I reached over and pulled her dress out for her.

"Daddy, that's how I got my first black eye."

Daddy said, "How'd you get that other one, son?"

I said, "I put it back in for her, daddy."

SANDWICH IN MY POCKET

I had an ole uncle down there in Pahokee, Florida. His name was Uncle Ernest and he had a little gas station on the outskirts of town. It was a little Spur station. There's probably a million or more of 'em across the southern United States.

It was a nice little station, 'ceptin' it didn't have indoor plumbin'. In other words, it didn't have a toilet on the inside. But, no matter, he had 'em a real nice one on the outside. It was a three-holer, triple "A" regulation unit, as they say.

One day, Uncle Ernest caught old T.T. fishing in one of them holes. It was the middle hole, if I recall correctly. Yeah! He had him a fishin' pole just a jiggin'.

Uncle Ernest hollored, "T. T., what on Earth are you a'doin'?"

T. T. shouted back, "Uncle Ernest, I dropped my jacket over in there and I'm a-tryin' to fish it out'a there."

Uncle Ernest said, "You ain't gonna wear it are you?"

T. T. said, "Naw sir, but I got a biscuit in the pocket."

PAINTIN' UNDER THIS ONE

One day me and ol' Randall Kemp was a-playin' 'round a junk pile out behind Uncle Ernest's Little Spur station, and, by chance, we happened 'cross an old Majestic radio that someone had discarded. Finding that was like findin' a buried treasure to us, and it gave me an idea.

I decided to get even with Miss Armstrong for slappin' me, and makin' me stutter for the rest of my life. (I'll tell you that story later on.)

So, we went to work and took the speaker out of that old

radio and installed it in one of the holes in that regulation outhouse. Then, we secretly borrowed a microphone and transmitter we used in our FFA class at school We wired it to that old Majestic radio speaker in the sh-sh-sh-outhouse, and waited patiently for Miss Armstrong to show up.

Now, Miss Armstrong was a regular customer at Uncle Ernest's little gas station, I mean, she was there every day, whether she needed anything or not. An, if you ask me, I think her and Uncle Ernest had a little thing goin', you know what I mean. Now, I didn't know that for a fact, but I always thought it, especially when I got up old enough to know what I was a-thinkin' 'bout.

Her routine was the same thing every day. She'd pull up in that old beat up car of hers and say, "Young man, fill 'er up, check my oil, check my tires, clean the windshield, front and back, and whisk it out."

And I'd say, "Miss Armstrong, I did that the day before and the day before that."

And she'd say, "Young man, you shut your mouth and do as you're told."

With those partin' words, she'd go inside and start into stuffin' candy bars down her heck. She'd have herself three or four Baby Ruths. A couple of Paydays, 'bout a dozen Banana Fingers, cheese crackers—I'd lose count of the Moon Pies. And then she'd down four or five of those little grapettes and top it all off with an R.C. Cola. She'd drink it down a little ways first, and then fill it back up to the top with some of those Tom Toasted peanuts, and shake it up 'til it started fizzin' real good.

Next, she'd squirt that wonderful concoction right down her neck. And in 'bout 15 minutes, she'd waddle out to the little outhouse. Now folks, that was the way it was, day in and day out.

One day, after we had installed the speaker in one of the outhouse holes, she pulled into the station like she owned the place and started into her routine. Me and Randall watches her from out of the corner of our eyes. And sure 'nuff, in 'bout 15 minutes she gingerly waddled out to the outhouse for some relief.

I looked at Randall and said, "This is it, Randall! This is it!" We raced for the microphone and since I could talk better than he could, I told him that I would do the announcin'. He agreed.

We gave her enough time to get comfortably settled down, and a chance to browse through a few pages of the latest issue of the Sears and Robuck catalog.

Then I spoke into the microphone loud and clear.

"M-M-M-Miss Armstrong. Would you m-m-mind movin' over to the next hole? I'm a p-p-p-aintin' under this one."

BEEF

- ◆ Beef Tips Over Rice
- ◆ Italian Meatloaf
- ◆ Beef Pot Roast
- ◆ Swiss Steak
- ◆ Chicken Fried Steak with Gravy
- ◆ Beef Brisket
- ◆ Savory Beef Stew
- ◆ Short Ribs
- ◆ Chinese Pepper Steak

Beef Tips Over Rice

1 pound sirloin steak, cubed, sprinkled with
    unseasoned tenderizer seasoning
1 medium onion, chopped
2 cloves garlic, minced
2 tablespoons olive oil
1 small can of mushrooms or 8-10 fresh ones
1/2 cup white wine
2 teaspoons beef base
Salt and fresh pepper to taste
1 tablespoon parsley flakes
1 tablespoon cornstarch
1/2 cup cold water
Hot cooked rice

Brown cubed steak, onion and garlic in olive oil in a large heavy skillet. Add mushrooms, wine, beef base, salt, pepper and parsley. Let simmer 15 or 20 minutes until meat is done, then dissolve cornstarch in water then let thicken. Takes just a few minutes. Serve over hot cooked rice.

Italian Meat Loaf

3 slices white bread
3 slices rye bread
1-1/4 cups beef stock
4 tablespoons minced onion
1 tablespoon prepared mustard
2 teaspoons salt
1/2 teaspoon parsley flakes
1/8 teaspoon black pepper
Cheese
2 eggs
2 pounds ground beef
1 tablespoon butter

Break white and rye bread into pieces in large mixing bowl. Add beef stock and onion. Let stand for 10 minutes. With fork, mash bread pieces and beat mixture well. Add mustard, salt, parsley flakes, pepper, cheese, eggs. Beat well with a fork. Add beef, mix thoroughly. Pack into oiled 9 x 5 inch loaf pan. Dot top with butter. Bake in 375 degree oven for 60-70 minutes. Makes 8 servings.

Beef Pot Roast

Chuck roast, 4 pounds
Salt and pepper
Flour, enough to coat meat
3 cloves minced garlic
1/4 cup olive oil
3 medium sized potatoes, quartered
2 medium sized onions, quartered (secured w/
       toothpick)
3-4 carrots, sliced
Water
Milk

Tenderize, salt and pepper chuck roast on both sides. Flour and brown the roast in minced garlic and shall amount of olive oil over medium heat. Once browned on both sides, place roast in oven glass dish with cover or a deep iron skillet.

Before covering, add potatoes, carrots and onions to dish along with juices from browning. Cover and cook slow on 300 degrees for 2 to 2-1/2 hours, depending on size of roast. Pour off drippings, add flour, water and milk to make a tasty gravy. The garlic makes this recipe. Serves 6-8 people.

Swiss Steak

Round steak (1-1/2 to 2 inches thick)
Meat Tenderizer
Worcestershire sauce
Catsup
Green pepper rings
Large onion rings
3 bacon slices, uncooked

    Sprinkle meat on both sides with tenderizer, piercing with a fork. Place steak in a 3 quarter rectangular baking dish. Heavily sprinkle meat with Worcestershire sauce, then spread thickly with catsup. Evenly distribute the pepper and onion rings; top with sliced bacon.
    Cover the dish tightly and bake at 250 degrees for 4 hours. About 45 minutes before the meat is done, remove cover and let brown. The gravy will be generous and delicious. If you desire thicker gravy, remove meat and blend in a small amount of flour. Serves 6 to 8.

Chicken Fried Steak with Gravy

1 pound round steak, 1/2 inch thick
Salt and freshly ground pepper
1 egg
1/3 cup milk
All-purpose flour
Vegetable oil or shortening

    Trim fat and gristle from meat. Place between slices of waxed paper and pound with meat mallet until fibers are broken down and meat is thinned. Cut into pieces about the size of your palm. Season both sides with salt and pepper.

Beat egg and milk together lightly. Pat flour into meat, dip into egg, then into flour again.

In a large heavy skillet, heat 1/4 inch oil or shortening to 400 degrees. Place steaks in hot fat; turn heat to low (about 310 degrees). Cook 5 to 10 minutes on first side until golden brown. Turn with spatula; cook 10 minutes on other side until browned. Drain on paper towel and keep warm in oven while making gravy. Omit egg if you prefer a lighter crust.

Steak Gravy:
3 tablespoons flour
2 cups milk
Salt and pepper to taste

Pour off fat from skillet, leaving thin film on bottom. Add flour; cook, stirring over medium heat until browned. Add milk all at once. Continue to cook, stirring until gravy thickens and is reduced. Taste for additional salt and pepper. Serve separately. Serves 4.

Beef Brisket

2-1/2 to 3 pounds well-trimmed boneless, beef brisket
Salt to taste
1/4 cup liquid smoke
1 teaspoon onion salt
1 teaspoon garlic salt

Sprinkle brisket with regular salt and place on a large piece of foil. Set in a shallow dish or pan and pour liquid smoke over meat. Seal foil and refrigerate overnight. Remove brisket from refrigerator, sprinkle with onion salt and garlic salt.

Reseal foil, bake at 250 degrees for 5 hours or until done. Slice thin and serve with smoky sauce.

Savory Beef Stew

2 pounds lean beef for stewing, cut into 1 inch cubes
1/4 cup oil
1-1/2 cups chopped onions
1 16 ounce can tomatoes, undrained and chopped
3 tablespoons quick tapioca
3 beef bouillon cubes
1 cup water
1 clove garlic, minced
1 tablespoon dried parsley flakes
2-1/2 teaspoons salt
1/2 teaspoon pepper
1 bay leaf
6 medium carrots, cut in strips
3 medium potatoes, cut into quarters
1/2 cup celery, sliced

Slowly brown meat in oil in a large skillet. Add onion, tomatoes, tapioca, bouillon cubes, water, garlic, parsley, salt, pepper and bay leaf; bring to a boil. Remove from skillet and place in a 3 quart casserole.

Cover and bake at 350 degrees for 1-1/2 hours. Add remaining ingredients and continue to bake for 30 to 45 minutes or until vegetables are tender. Yield 5 to 6 servings.

Short Ribs

2 pounds beef short ribs
Small piece of fat
1 20 ounce can tomatoes

1/2 teaspoon pepper
1 cup water
1/8 teaspoon ground ginger
3 tablespoons onion, chopped
2 bay leaves
1 tablespoon horseradish

Cut ribs into serving pieces. Melt a small piece of fat in a heavy skillet and brown ribs on all sides. Place meat in a 2 quart casserole. Combine remaining ingredients and pour mixture over meat

Bake covered at 350 degrees for 1-1/2 to 2 hours or until ribs are very tender. Serves 4.

Chinese Pepper Steak

1-1/2 pounds sirloin, 1-inch thick
1 teaspoon salt
1/2 teaspoon pepper
1/4 cup Crisco oil
1 clove garlic, crushed
1 teaspoon ginger
3 large green peppers, sliced
2 large onions, sliced
1/4 cup soy sauce
1/2 teaspoon sugar
1/2 cup beef bouillon
1 can water chestnuts, sliced
1 tablespoon cornstarch

1/4 cup cold water
4 green onions, cut into 1-inch pieces

Cut steak into 1-inch strips and season with salt and pepper. Heat oil in skillet; add garlic and ginger. Saute until garlic is golden. Add steak slices and brown for 2 minutes.

Remove meat from skillet; add peppers and on ions and saute until tender. Place meat back in skillet; add all other ingredients and heat.

Serve immediately over fluffy rice or noodles.

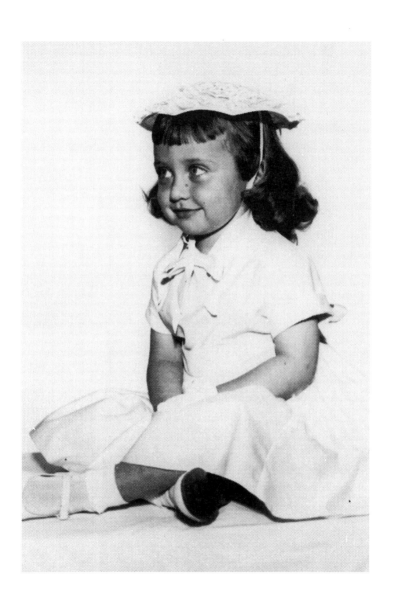

Pam, 4 years

SECTION IX

Mel's Favorite ... Pork

Mel and his youngest daughter, Hannah, 7

CLEO AND HER ASP

One summer night I was watchin' the gas station for Uncle Ernest. He said he had to go and deliver some kerosene to a lady. How he knew that, I didn't rightly know, 'cause we didn't have a phone, and it wasn't cold either. It was dog days.

Anyway, he left me there all by myself, and I was scared to death. Heck, I was only 11 years old. This was in the days 'fore they had finished buildin' the levee around Lake Okeechobee, and you could look out the window of the little gas station and all you could see was water. Water, water, everywhere. Dark, scary water.

And on the other side of the road was the beginnin' of the Everglades, and it was scary over there, too, 'cause there were things over there that would get choooo! There were mosquitoes over there as big as buzzards, and all kinda bugs; red bugs, ticks, gnats, horse flies, house flies, blind gnats. I could go on and on 'bout bugs. There were reptiles of every kind: alligators, crocodiles, snakes, big snakes, snakes as big an' round as your leg and 20-foot long. There were black snakes, brown snakes, green snakes, tree snakes, copper headed rattle moccasins. Now, that's the worse kind, them copper headed rattle moccasins.

There were whip snakes, and them whip snakes would chase you, and if they ever caught you, they'd put a whuppin' on you wors'er than your pappy could. One never did get after me, tho, but if it had'da, I'd showed it the state of Florida and some parts of Georgia and Tennessee, if I'd had to. There were leaper snakes, the kind that stay up in oak trees, and if you happened to be walkin' 'neath one of them trees where they're lurkin', they'd leapt out and land right on top of your head.

There were pythons, cobras, boas, adders and puff adders, all them adder family snakes. There were rat snakes, chicken snakes, anaconda, coral snakes, garter snakes, gopher snakes, bull snakes, and asp snakes. Yes, asps. The kind that bit ol' Cleo.

Y'all remember old Cleo, don't you. Well, if you learned anything in school you should remember that she was the one that drove old Marc Anthony bananas, and caused him to kill himself. Then she felt so badly 'bout it, she let her pet asp out of its basket and aggravated it 'til it bit her and she keeled over dead.

And while we're talkin' 'bout asps, here's somethin' else you should know. If you go to the pet shop and buy yourself a pet asp and you happen to be out in them Everglades a-crawlin' your pet asp along, and you'all happen to run into a wild asp -- that wild asp will bite your asp.

And the moral of this story is, you better keep your asp at home.

PORK

♦ Spare Ribs
♦ Cuban Roast Pork
♦ Pork Chops and Rice
♦ Pork Chops Creole
♦ Baked Ham
♦ Parmesan Breaded Chops
♦ Ham Loaf
♦ Pork Sausage Sweet Potato Apple Casserole

♦ Mel's Fried Pork Chops
♦ Sausage Pie

Spare Ribs

2 sides of baby ribs
Salt and pepper
1 egg
3 tablespoons milk
Self-rising flour
Cooking oil

Boil ribs until tender in salty water; take out, pepper them good; beat 1 egg. Add 3 tablespoons milk and salt to taste. Roll ribs in egg and milk, then roll them good in self-rising flour. Fry in real hot grease. (Cooking oil preferred).

Cuban Roast Pork

2 garlic buds
6 pound pork loin roast
1 teaspoon salt
1/4 teaspoon pepper
4 tablespoons oregano
2/3 cup fresh lime juice

Cut garlic into slivers; make slits all over the roast and insert garlic. Combine salt, pepper and oregano. Rub this over the meat. Place fat side up on a rack pan in 450 degree oven and cook uncovered 30-35 minutes to the pound. If a thermometer is used, it should read 185 degrees. When pork begins to brown, baste frequently with lime juice. (This roast has a slight garlic flavor with a crisp, tart crust). *Serve with spiced crabapples.*

Pork Chops and Rice

Vegetable oil
4-6 pork chops
Salt and pepper to taste
2/3 cup chopped green pepper
2/3 cup chopped onion
2 10-1/2 ounce cans chicken soup
2/3 cup uncooked long-grain rice
1/2 cup hot water

Heat oven to 350 degrees. Heat vegetable oil in skillet; brown pork chops. Sprinkle lightly with salt and pepper. Remove chops to shallow baking dish placing 1 layer deep. In same skillet lightly saute green pepper and onion. Sprinkle very lightly with salt and pepper and place over pork chops. Mix together soup, uncooked rice and water. Pour over and around pork chops. Cover tightly and bake for 1-1/2 hours.

Pork Chops Creole

3 tablespoons all-purpose flour
1/4 teaspoon salt
Freshly ground pepper, to taste
4 pork loin chops, cut 1 inch thick, trimmed of fat
3 tablespoons vegetable oil
3 medium carrots, pared and sliced (1/4" thick)

1 large tomato, skinned and chopped
1/2 cup minced onion
1/4 cup (1/4 inch sliced) green pepper
1/2 cup (1/4 inch sliced) celery
1 clove garlic, minced
1/4 teaspoon dried rosemary
2 cups vegetable cocktail juice

Heat oven to 375 degrees. In large plastic bag, combine flour, salt and pepper; add chops. Twist bag closed and shake until chops are well coated on all sides. In a large heavy skillet, heat oil and lightly brown coated chops.

Remove chops to a 2 quart casserole. Place vegetables over chops. Sprinkle with rosemary and salt and pepper to taste. Pour vegetable cocktail juice around chops.
Bake covered for 2 hours. Remove cover and bake 15 minutes more.

Baked Ham with Fruit Glaze

1 (5-6 pound) boneless ham
1 can purple plums
3/4 cup orange juice
1/2 cup brown sugar
1 teaspoon dry mustard
1/4 teaspoon cloves
2 teaspoons grated orange peel

Place ham in preheated oven at 325 degrees in

shallow baking pan. Combine the plums, juice, sugar, mustard, cloves and orange peel. Heat until sugar has dissolved.

Bake ham for 1 hour, then pour some of the marinade over the ham, saving half for basting and for a sauce. Continue to bake for 20 minutes and when done, remove from pan to serving platter and garnish with some purple plums.

This sauce is excellent thickened with a little cornstarch and served with the ham at the table.

Parmesan Breaded Pork Chops

1 cup seasoned bread crumbs
3 tablespoons Parmesan cheese
Salt and pepper
1 egg
2 tablespoons milk
8 pork chops
1/2 tablespoon butter

Combine bread crumbs, Parmesan cheese, salt and pepper. Beat egg and milk in flat dish. Dip chops in crumbs, then egg mixture, then again in crumbs. Melt butter in baking dish and place chops in dish.

Bake at 325 degrees for 1 hour, turning after first 30 minutes. If chops are thick or not too brown, cook longer. (To use with 4 chops, reduce crumbs to 2/3 cup.) Serves 4-8.

Ham Loaf

1-1/2 pounds ground ham
1-1/2 pounds ground beef

1/2 cup milk
1 cup cracker crumbs
2 eggs
1 onion, chopped
Black pepper

Combine all ingredients. Mix well and shape into a loaf. Bake at 325-350 degrees for about 1-1/2 hours. Let ham bake 30 minutes before basting.

Ham Sauce for Loaf:
3/4 cup brown sugar
1/2 cup vinegar
1/2 cup water
1 teaspoon mustard

Bring to a boil and boil for 5 minutes. Baste ham often.

Pork Sausage Sweet Potato Apple Casserole

3 medium sweet potatoes
3 medium tart apples
1/2 cup brown sugar
1/8 teaspoon allspice
1/2 teaspoon salt
1 pound pork sausage links
2 tablespoons drippings
1/4 cup boiling water

Boil sweet potatoes until tender; pare and cut in thick slices. Lay half the slices in greased casserole. Core unpeeled applies and cut across into 1/8 inch slices. Put half the slices on top of the potato slices. Sprinkle with brown sugar mixed with allspice and salt. Add remaining potatoes and apples.

Fry sausage links 10 minutes and place in casserole. Mix drippings and water; pour water all over. Bake in moderate oven (375 degrees) for 40 minutes. Serves 4.

Mel's Fried Pork Chops

8 pork chops
Salt and pepper
1 cup plain flour, less or more depending on the need
1 cup vegetable oil

Salt and pepper pork chops and dredge with plain flour. In a large skillet pour 1 cup vegetable oil. Let oil get hot on medium fire, then place pork chops in the skillet.

When they are browned on the bottom side, turn'em over and brown the top side.

Mel's Sausage Pie

1 tablespoon drippings
1 pound pork sausage
2 applies, sliced
2 onions, sliced
1 tablespoon flour
1 cup stock or water
Mashed potatoes (homemade)
Melted butter

Heat drippings in a skillet; add sausages and cook until browned all over. Remove sausages and keep hot. To the same pan add apples and onions, adding more fat if needed and brown lightly. Remove applies and onions and keep hot. Pour off all but 2 tablespoons of the fat. Stir in flour and brown it. Stir in stock or water and cook until blended and smooth. Over this, pour the thickened stock.

Cover with a crust of the hot mashed potatoes, having this in peaks. Lightly brush top of surface with melted butter. Brown in moderate oven (350 degrees). Serves 6.

SECTION X

Mel's Favorite ... Game and Wild Stuff

"Chef" Mel

HOW MANY CHICKENS IN THE SACK

One Sunday, the preacher was comin' to our house for Sunday dinner. It was our turn to feed him, and the preacher loved chicken, especially chicken and dumplin's. Well, we had plenty of dumplin's but we'd run out of chicken, so mama sent me over to ol' man Pooles to buy a couple of nice fat hens. She warned me as I left,

"Don't you come back here with any skinny chickens, Melvin. Do you hear me?"

"Yes ma'am, mama," I hollered as I trotted off down the road to ol' man Pooles' place. "I heard you — I know what to do."

Ol' man Poole had a nice flock of chickens, "'bout a hundred and fifty," he said. And they were all Dominickers (Dominiques) as we called them. I remembered what mama had told me, "Don't you come back here with any skinny chickens."

Well sir, them chickens all looked alike to me. They all seemed to be about the same size. And it was right then and there that I realized you can't tell how fat a chicken is just by looking at it. Have you ever seen a chicken with a fat face? If you have, come and get me so's I can go and look at it, too.

No sir, you got to feel of a chicken to know how fat it really is. I felt all hundred and fifty of ol' man Poole's chickens, and finally decided on the fattest two of the flock. I paid him a dollar and a half for them squawkin' fowls, put 'em in a croaker sack and headed for home.

Now I had spent a lot of time feeling them chickens and I needed to make it up so I decided to take a short cut home, by

T. T. And he said,

"Hey Melvin, what you got in the sack?"

I told him,

"I got some f-f-f-fat chickens in the sack, T. T."

He looked the sack over real good. I could tell he was studying, and then he asked me,

"Melvin, if I can tell you how many chickens you got in the sack, will you give me one?"

I knew I was in trouble; I had to get home just as sure as them chickens were a-squawkin'.

So I decided to tell old T. T. the truth, even though he'd never believe the truth. And I said,

"T. T., if you can tell me how many chickens I got in this sack, I'll give you both of 'em."

T. T. said, "Six."

Mama made some real good dumplin's with those two fat chickens.

Preacher said, "'Bout the best the good Lord had ever blessed us with, don't you agree, Melvin?"

And I said, "A-A-Amen."

GAME AND WILD STUFF

- Fried Quail
- Quail Pie
- Venison Roast
- Venison Steaks
- Venison Soup
- Roasted Wild Duck
- Fried Rabbit

♦ Basted Doves
♦ Fried Frog Legs
♦ Tennessee Smothered Squirrel

Fried Quail

Dress Quail and split down the back leaving the breast intact. Flatten out each bird with breast down and dust with salt and pepper on both sides. Roll each bird in flour. Place birds in skillet containing hot grease. The grease should come halfway up on the birds. Brown well on all sides, then cover the skillet and turn down the heat to low simmer.

Cook 30 to 40 minutes and serve. Drippings can be used to make cream gravy to go with mashed potatoes.

Quail Pie

6 quail
Salt and pepper
Flour
Grease
6 slices carrot
1 stalk celery
2 slices onion
1 bay leaf
Sprig of parsley
1/4 teaspoon peppercorn
Lemon juice

Remove breasts and legs; season with salt and pepper and roll in flour. Fry in grease. Add vegetables and peppercorn; cook 5 minutes. Cut backs into pieces and cover with cold water, cooking slowly for one hour. Drain liquid from vegetables and thicken with flour. Dust with salt, pepper and lemon juice. Make biscuit dough for pie and fill with meat and broth. Put on top crust and bake 10 minutes at 450 degrees. Reduce heat to 350 degrees and bake until done.

Venison Roast

1 roast of venison
Lard
6 bacon strips
1 cup butter
Salt and pepper to taste
Garlic cloves, minced or whole
1 cup hot water
1/2 cup sour cream
1/2 cup sweet cream
1/2 cup flour

Rub well-trimmed roast with lard and brown in skillet. Cover generously with salt and pepper and place in roasting pan. Layer bacon over roast. Add garlic cloves to your liking. Pour 1 cup hot water over meat, cover and bake at 350 degrees (about 1/2 hour per pound).

Baste during cooking. Remove about 30 minutes prior to completion and make gravy, if desired, from sour cream, sweet cream, flour and meat drippings. Return meat to pan and pan to oven and bake at 325 degrees for 30 minutes, basting roast with gravy.

Venison Steaks

Venison steaks, sliced 1/2 inch thick (loin or ham cut)
Unseasoned meat tenderizer
Flour

1/4 cup milk
Bacon drippings
Salt

Remove all tissue from venison. A properly dressed deer will have no gamey taste. Cut into very small pieces (about the size of a silver dollar). Sprinkle each steak with tenderizer and then beat with mallet 'til tender. Dip into flour, then milk, then flour again.

Fry in iron skillet in oil or drippings until brown, then place in oven for additional 1 hour or less. Do not overcook, as they will become tough. Salt after cooking. *Serve with bread and gravy.*

Venison Soup

1 (3 pound) venison roast
4 cups cold water
1 tablespoon salt
1-1/2 quarts water
1 bunch celery hearts (sliced)
2 cups tomatoes, diced
3 medium potatoes, cubed
4 onions, cubed
1 clove garlic
1 bay leaf
1 green, red or yellow pepper, diced small
1 tablespoon parsley
Salt and pepper

Soak roast in cold salt water overnight. Discard water and put meat in 1-1/2 quarts water. Simmer for 2-1/2 hours;

remove and cool meat. Place in refrigerator overnight.

Next day, skim off fat, simmer 2 hours; 20 minutes before meat is done, add celery, tomatoes, potatoes, onions, garlic, bay leaf and small diced peppers. (This gives it additional taste and color). Add parley. Season to taste with salt and pepper. If necessary, thicken with a little flour. Serves 6 to 8.

Wild Duck

Wild ducks, cleaned
Adolph's Meat Tenderizer
Salt and pepper
Garlic cloves or powder
Apples, quartered
Onions, quartered
Celery stalks
Bacon
Lemon slices
7-8 cans consomme, undiluted
Flour
2 bay leaves
1 cup burgundy or Sherry
1 cup whipping cream

Sprinkle ducks with tenderizer, refrigerate overnight. Rub whole birds inside and out with salt, pepper and fresh minced garlic, or powder, if you must. Stuff breast cavities with apple, onion and celery; place ducks in large roaster and strip with bacon. Add lemon slices.

Pour consomme into roaster (do not pour over ducks) to cover half the birds. Roast, covered to retain juices, at 300-325 degrees for 3 to 3-1/2 hours or until barely tender.

Do not overcook; add more consomme if needed. It may take 7 to 8 cans, depending on number of ducks. Drizzle any moisture which collects over ducks. Remove ducks; halve. Discard bacon, vegetables and lemon slices. Add additional consomme, if necessary (depending on amount of gravy required) and thicken with a small amount of flour. Add bay leaves. Add duck halves, breast side down and baste with wine.

Simmer on top of stove about 1 hour; continue to baste frequently. Turn off heat; just before serving, stir cream, into gravy. Remove bay leaves. The meat should be juicy, tender and falling off the bone.

Fried Rabbit

Rabbit
Salt and pepper
Flour
Cooking oil

Salt, pepper and flour cut-up rabbit and drop into a heavy skillet with medium hot cooking oil. Brown rabbit on both sides. Cover skillet and simmer until done, about 30 minutes.

Basted Doves

10-12 cleaned doves
Salt and pepper

4 tablespoons butter, divided
1/2 cup water
1/4 cup sherry

Salt and pepper the cleaned doves. Melt about 2 tablespoons of butter in an oven-proof skillet. Put doves into skillet, breast side down; sear. Turn and sear on other side.

Add about 2 more tablespoons of butter and the water. Cover and bake at 325 degrees about 1 hour or more (until tender), basting 3 or 4 times. Add sherry in the final minutes.

Fried Frog Legs

Soak frogs' legs in equal amounts of salt water and milk for 1 hour. Drain; pat dry. Shake in bag of seasoned flour. Saute in hot oil or butter until tender.

Serve with lemon or lime wedges and homemade country fries.

Tennessee Smothered Squirrel

Squirrels, cut into serving pieces
Salt and pepper
1 medium onion, chopped
1/4 cup celery, chopped
1 beef bouillon cube
3 tablespoons butter
Flour
1/2 teaspoon curry powder

1/2 cup orange juice
1 teaspoon cornstarch

Salt and pepper squirrels and place with onion, celery and bouillon cube in a pot. Cover with water, bring to a boil, then turn to low heat and simmer for 1-1/2 hours.

Remove little critters, roll in flour and brown in heavy skillet in the butter. Add onion-celery broth, curry powder, orange juice and cornstarch. Cook for 5 minutes over a medium heat, stirring constantly.

You can also fry the squirrels using the same recipe as the Fried Quail, adding garlic powder.

SECTION XI

Mel's Favorite ... Sauces

Time to cook the grits!

WHEN THE CIRCUS CAME
TO PAHOKEE

O ne pretty fall day, with a cool breeze comin' in off Lake Okeechobee, a little circus came to Pahokee. It wasn't a very big circus, for it only consisted of one big tent. They had a couple of shaggy old lions that looked dead old to me; I couldn't see their teeth, but they could still growl pretty good when the ring master cracked the whip into their faces.

They had two of the biggest horses I'd ever seen, and little midgets did tricks on their backs as they whirled around the ring. They had a few clowns and chimps runnin' 'round in the bleachers scarin' the people half to death. They also had some little dogs jumpin' through hoops and stuff like that.

But the grandest of them all were the two big elephants. They did all manner of tricks. They could rare up on their hind legs or stand up on their front legs. We ooohed and awwwed as they tread atop red barrels with miniature ponies on their backs.

All in all, it was great entertainment for a little town like Pahokee, Florida, in 1943.

The very first night the circus was in town, you might know it, one of the elephants got loose and wandered along the levee all night, and wound up the next morning in the back of Miss Armstrong's house, feasting on the cabbage in her vegetable garden.

Miss Armstrong was up early that morning, like always, makin' biscuits and gravy. She was washin' her hands at the kitchen sink when she looked out the window and spotted the huge grey animal in her garden. Well, sir, she liked to have dropped her teeth. She raced for the telephone and called the

122

Pahokee Police Department.

"Pahokee Police Department, Can I help you?" came a cheerful voice.

She said, "Who is this?"

"Sgt. Justice, ma'am, Sgt. Buford P. Justice. Who is this?"

"This is Miss Armstrong, Buford," she cried. "You know where I live on Bacon Point Road?"

"Yes I do, Miss Armstrong. Know exactly where you live. Why?"

"Because there's a large grey animal of some kind in my garden."

Now, Miss Armstrong had never seen a real, live elephant before and panicked. She didn't quite know how to describe what her eyes were seeing.

"What kind of animal you lookin' at, Miss Armstrong?" inquired Buford.

"Well, I don't rightly know, Buford. It's real tall and grey lookin', and it's-----."

"Wait a minute," Buford interrupted. "Let me write that down. You say it's tall and grey lookin'. What's it doin'?"

"Well, right now, it's pullin' up my cabbage with its tail."

"Pullin' up my cabbage with its tail," Buford muttered to himself as he jotted down what she'd told him. "Miss Armstrong, will you please repeat what you just said?"

"It's pullin' up my cabbage with its tail," she repeated.

"That's what I thought you said." There was a moment of silence, then Buford came back with, "What's it doin' with the cabbage, Miss Armstrong?"

"Buford, if I told you...you wouldn't believe me."

SAUCES

♦ Creole Sauce
♦ Mama's Lemon Sauce
♦ Tartar Sauce
♦ Hollandaise Sauce
♦ Steak Sauce
♦ Spanish Sauce
♦ Beef Sauce
♦ Po' Boys Gravy
♦ Mel's Thanksgiving Giblet Gravy
♦ Quick Onion Sauce for Steaks

Creole Sauce

1 cup chopped green pepper
2 cups chopped onions
1 cup mushrooms (pieces)
4 cups chopped celery
1/2 teaspoon garlic salt
1 tablespoon chili powder
1 can tomato sauce

Saute peppers, onion, mushrooms and celery in small amount of oil; add garlic salt, chili powder and tomato sauce. Simmer until chopped vegetables are done.

Short ribs of beef are wonderful baked in this sauce. To do this, dust 4 pounds short ribs with garlic salt, put on rack in broiler pan. Brown slightly in oven. Then add above sauce to short ribs, return to oven for about 45 minutes at 350 degrees. Serve with plain rice or Mexican rice listed in this cookbook.

Mama's Lemon Sauce

1/2 cup butter
1 egg, well beaten
1 cup sugar
3 tablespoons lemon juice
1/4 cup water
Grated rind of 1 lemon

Combine all ingredients. Cook over medium heat, stirring constantly until boiling. Serve warm. May be refrigerated and reheated. Yields 1-1/2 cups.

Tartar Sauce

1 cup mayonnaise or cooked dressing
1/4 cup pickles, chopped
1 teaspoon minced onion
1 tablespoon capers (optional)
1 teaspoon chopped ripe olives
1 tablespoon minced fresh parsley
1 hard cook egg, chopped
1 teaspoon chopped green pepper
1 teaspoon prepared mustard
1/4 dried tarragon (optional)
Lemon juice

Blend all ingredients and add lemon juice to thin slightly and point up flavors. Makes about 1-1/2 cups.

Hollandaise Sauce

1 stick butter
4 egg yolks
Dash of salt
1/4 cup lemon juice
1/4 cup whipping cream

Melt butter in double boiler. Stir in egg yolks and salt. Add lemon juice while beating with an electric mixer. After mixture begins to thicken, remove from heat. Beat in whipping cream. This can be made ahead of time, refrigerated and reheated. When reheating, beat with electric mixer to avoid lumps.

Steak Sauce

1/2 cup oil
Accent
1/4 cup Kitchen Bouquet
Juice of 1 lemon
Zest of 1 orange
Salt and pepper
Garlic to taste
Charcoal seasoning

Combine all ingredients. Brush on steaks and broil.

Spanish Sauce for Baked Fish

1/2 cup fresh light olive oil
5 cloves garlic, c hopped finely
2 green peppers, chopped
3 onions, coarsely chopped
1 (1 lb. 12 oz.) can tomatoes
1 (10-1/2 oz.) can tomato puree
2 Bay leaves
1/4 teaspoon oregano
1-1/2 teaspoons Worcestershire sauce
Juice of one lime

In saucepan, heat olive oil and cook garlic and green peppers until latter are almost tender. Add onion; cook until tender, but not browned.

Stir in tomatoes, tomato puree, bay leaves, oregano, Worcestershire sauce, lime juice and salt and pepper to taste. Simmer until thickened and well blended, about 20 minutes, stirring occasionally. Makes about 2-1/2 cups sauce. *Great for mackerel or snapper.*

Beef Sauce

1 cup chili sauce
2 tablespoons bacon fat
3 tablespoons brown sugar
1 cup water
Juice of two lemons

1 teaspoon paprika
1 tablespoon Worcestershire
3 teaspoons vinegar
1/4 teaspoon celery salt
1 teaspoon salt
1/3 cup grated onion

Combine all ingredients and stir to blend. Pour half over meat, save half. Bake uncovered at 325 degrees for 45 minutes. Serve hot sauce with meat.

Po' Boys Country Gravy

2 cups milk
1/4 cup flour
1/4 cup drippings
Salt and pepper

This is milk gravy made after frying chicken, salt pork, or sausage. Make a smooth thin paste with a little of the milk and flour. Add paste to hot drippings, stirring constantly.

Add remaining milk, stir and cook until gravy is smooth and thickened. Season to taste.

Mel's Thanksgiving Giblet Gravy

Always requested at Thanksgiving! The kids love it!

Chop cooked giblets fine and save in broth in which they were cooked. Skim off extra fat and leave some for gravy. Add 1/4 cup flour and 1/4 meal.

Add chopped hard boiled eggs. Gradually add broth until smooth and desired consistency is reached.

Add giblets and salt and pepper taste. For thinner gravy, add more liquid.

Quick Onion Sauce for Steaks

Heat 1 can ready to serve onion soup. Blend in a little flour to thicken it and cook a few minutes. If desired add a little grated cheese just before serving. You can also saute a few onions and add for extra flavor.

SECTION XII

Mel's...Dressings & Stuffings

Mel with his mother, Richard, and Linda

DRESSINGS AND STUFFINGS

- ◆ Oyster Stuffing
- ◆ Chicken and Corn Bread Dressing
- ◆ Plain Ol' Corn Bread Dressing
- ◆ Bread Stuffing
- ◆ Celery Onion Stuffing for Fish
- ◆ Potato Stuffing
- ◆ Wild Rice and Mushroom Stuffing
- ◆ Orange Stuffing for Ducks & Geese
- ◆ Corn Stuffing for Poultry
- ◆ Sweet Potato Stuffing

Oyster Stuffing

My home state, Florida, is well known for its Oysters, especially the Apalachicola oysters. The following recipe is one of my favorite oyster stuffing recipes:

6 tablespoons butter
1 pint oysters with liquid
1/4 cup minced onion
4 cups crumbled corn bread
3/4 teaspoon salt
2 lightly beaten eggs
1/4 teaspoon paprika
2 tablespoons minced parsley

Melt butter and saute onion until golden brown. Stir in all remaining ingredients. Toss lightly to mix. Cool before stuffing your turkey.

Chicken and Corn Bread Dressing

Livers, gizzards, necks and wings of 3 chickens
1 quart wheat bread, crumbled, (day old)
1/2 stalk celery, finely chopped
1 quart corn bread, crumbled (day old)
1 small bunch green onion tops, finely chopped
6 eggs, well beaten
4 cups chicken stock
1 green pepper, finely chopped

Start chicken cooking with 5 cups cold water and simmer until tender. Add 2 tablespoons butter or cooking oil, and 2 tablespoons water to chopped celery, onions and pepper and steam until tender.

Pull chicken from bones and chop fine. Add salt and pepper to taste. Now mix together all ingredients and bake at 350 degrees for 40 minutes. Great with pork chops or chicken.

Plain Ol' Corn Bread Dressing

1 quart corn bread crumbs
3/4 chopped celery
1 1/2 cup chopped onion
1 cup chicken livers diced
1 teaspoon black pepper
1 teaspoon sage or more to taste
2 hard boiled eggs
1/4 cup margarine
1 cup meat stock

1 can cream of celery soup
1 can cream of chicken soup
1 teaspoon poultry seasonings

Mix day old cornbread crumbs, sage, pepper, poultry seasonings and eggs together. Place remaining ingredients in saucepan and cook celery and onion until tender.

Add to first mixture with small amount of meat stock; if too dry, add cream of celery and cream of chicken soup. Mix well with hands. Place in greased dish and sprinkle with paprika. Bake at 375 degrees for 45 minutes or until done.

Bread Stuffing for Fish

6 tablespoons butter or margarine
1/2 cup diced celery
1/4 cup diced shallots or mild-flavored onions
1/4 teaspoon dried thyme
1/8 teaspoon sage
1/8 teaspoon garlic powder
Salt and pepper to taste
4 cups bread crumbs made by grating or crumbling
    day old bread
1 to 3 tablespoons fish fumet or chicken stock

Melt butter in large heavy skillet or pot. Add celery and shallots and cook a few minutes over medium heat, stirring frequently, until vegetables start to soften.

Stir in seasonings. Add bread crumbs and continue to stir until all ingredients are well mixed. Stir in just enough of the fish fumet to give a good consistency for stuffing.

Celery-Onion Stuffing for Fish

3 tablespoons shortening or margarine
1/4 cup chopped onion
1/4 cup chopped celery
2-1/2 cups toasted bread crumbs
2 tablespoons minced parsley
1 tablespoon lemon juice
1/2 teaspoon salt
1/4 teaspoon sage
3 tablespoons milk or water

Melt shortening in skillet; add onion and celery and saute together until tender. Pour over toasted bread crumbs, adding parsley, lemon juice, salt and sage. Add milk and mix well. Makes stuffing for 1 to 4-5 pound fish. *Toasted pine nuts will give this an extra flare if needed.*

Potato Stuffing

1/2 cup bacon or salt drippings
1 cup chopped onions
1/2 cup chopped celery
10 medium potatoes, cooked and diced
4 slices bread, crumbled
2 beaten eggs
1 tablespoon poultry seasoning
1 teaspoon salt
1/4 teaspoon pepper

1-1/2 teaspoon Accent

Melt fat in frying pan, add onions and celery; cook until soft but not brown. Combine remaining ingredients; add contents of frying pan and mix well. *Makes enough stuffing for one goose or two small ducklings.*

Wild Rice & Mushroom Stuffing

2 cups wild rice
Salted water
3 teaspoons chopped onion
3/4 cup sliced mushrooms
1/4 cup fat or salad oil
1 teaspoon salt
Dash of pepper

Wash rice and cover with salted water. Bring to a boil and cook until tender, about 20 minutes. Drain. Brown onion and mushrooms in hot fat. Mix with rice, salt and pepper. Makes enough for 4 to 5 pound bird. *You can also replace the mushrooms with chestnuts for a chestnut stuffing.*

Orange Stuffing

3/4 cup butter or margarine
1/2 cup chopped onion
1-1/2 cups chopped celery
1 cup boiling water
2 teaspoons salt
2 teaspoons poultry seasoning
1/2 teaspoon pepper
2 tablespoons grated orange rind
2 tablespoons minced parsley

2 quarts toasted bread crumbs
2 cups diced oranges

Saute onion in butter. Cook celery in water until tender. Add seasonings, orange rind, and parsley. Add to cooked onions with bread crumbs and oranges. Mix well and stuff goose or ducks. Makes stuffing for 2 ducks or a 10-12 pound goose.

Corn Stuffing for Poultry

2 cups canned corn, drained
2-1/2 cups bread crumbs
2 eggs
1 tablespoon finely minced green pepper
2/3 teaspoon salt
1/4 teaspoon pepper
2 tablespoons fat

Mix all ingredients thoroughly. If too dry, add a little chicken broth. If too moist, add a little more bread crumbs. Makes stuffing for 4 to 5 pound bird.

Sweet Potato Stuffing

6-8 sweet potatoes, cooked
Salt and pepper
1/2 cup melted butter
Orange juice or milk, as needed

Mash cooked sweet potatoes and season with salt, pepper and melted butter. Moisten with orange juice, or milk, and 1 slightly beaten egg for each 3 cups stuffing. Use with duck or turkey.

Mel's proud to be a 32nd ° Mason with Red Hat.

SECTION XIII

Mel's ... Fresh Vegetables

Mel, kids, sons-in-laws, and grandchildren

ASK THE LADY AT THE DESK

As a celebrity of sorts, I'm asked from time to time to come around to different places and give speeches, motivating speeches. And, being a stutterer, people like to know and hear me tell of my some degree of success, and to hear about some of the problems I've had to deal with. One day, I was asked to come down to a little rest home in Northern Arkansas, and I went and I took my guitar along with me, for I didn't know what to expect; I'd never been to an old folks home before.

I was with those wonderful senior citizens for about three hours, and let me tell you, we had a great time. We sang songs, told stories (I got some real douseys from some of them folks) and I had lunch with them and signed autographs.

Just before I had to leave and head back to Branson, one of the attendants asked me, "Mel, I want you to come with me up to the end of the hall and meet Aunt Nellie."

"Who's Aunt Nellie?" I asked.

"Aunt Nellie's the eldest of the home," he said.

"How old is she?" I inquired.

"She's 103 years old," he answered.

Somewhat awed by her age, I said, "Let's go."

I kissed a few folks and said good-bye to the others. Then me and the attendant walked to the end of a long hallway, and knocked on the door of the end room. A surprisingly strong voice said, "Come in."

We entered the room, and there she was, sitting up in her

bed watching the tube. She looked so pretty; someone had fixed her hair and it was almost blue. I had my guitar draped around my neck and I strummed an e-chord as I knelt beside the bed.

"Aunt Nellie, do you know who I am?" I asked.

She looked at me like I was some kind of a nut and said, "No, I don't know who you are, but if you'll go up to the end of the hall and take a left, and asked the lady at the desk, she'll tell you who you are."

Enough said.

Vegetables

We always had a garden. It was a way of life for most folk. We always had fresh veggies, and in south Florida, you could raise a garden year round.

♦ Okra and Tomatoes
♦ Okra Supreme
♦ Hog Jowls and Turnips
♦ Mama's Favorite Eggplant Casserole
♦ Eggplant Fritters
♦ Mashed Turnips
♦ Boiled Squash
♦ Deviled Beets
♦ Herbed Potatoes
♦ Stuffed Peppers

Okra and Tomatoes

2 pounds Okra
2 cups water
1 medium onion, sliced
1 tablespoon vinegar
1 teaspoon salt

2 tablespoons bacon drippings
1 16 ounce can stewed tomatoes
1/2 teaspoon sugar
1/2 teaspoon salt
1/8 teaspoon pepper

Wash okra well. Cut off tips and stem ends; cut okra crosswise into 1/2 inch slices. Combine okra, water, onion, vinegar, and 1 teaspoon salt. Cover and cook over medium-high heat for 15 minutes. Drain; cook over low heat until all moisture evaporates.

Add remaining ingredients; cook over medium heat, turning frequently, until brown. Serves 6 to 8 people.

Okra Supreme

2 medium potatoes, diced
5 cups sliced okra
1/2 cup cornmeal
1/2 cup vegetable oil
1/2 cup chopped green pepper
2 tablespoons chopped onion
1/3 cup chopped bacon, uncooked
Salt and pepper to taste

Combine potatoes, okra, and cornmeal; mix well. Cook in hot oil in a large skillet until golden brown, stirring occasionally. Add remaining ingredients; stir well.

Cover and cook about 5 minutes or until bacon is done. Serve hot. Serves 8 people.

Hog Jowls and Turnips

Hog jowls
Greens; turnips, mustard or kale
Salt and pepper to taste
Tabasco
Vinegar

Mustard, kale and turnip greens are cooked the same as spinach. Smoked hog jowl is cooked with greens. Season well with salt and pepper. Cook until tender, drain and serve on platter with meat in center.

Always, always serve with cornbread! Keep Tabasco and vinegar on the table.

Mama's Favorite Eggplant Casserole

My oldest daughter, Pam, likes to make this. It reminds her of her grandmother.

1 or 2 small eggplant
1 cup onion
1 egg
1 cup crackers
1 chicken bouillon cube
Dab of margarine
Cheese

Dice eggplant; bring to boil in water, then turn down to medium (about 10 minutes), and drain well when tender. Mash and add onion, egg, crackers, chicken bouillon and a dab of margarine. Bake 45 minutes at 350 degrees. Grate cheese and pour over eggplant 5 minutes before taking out.

Eggplant Fritters

Peel and cube eggplant. Cook in small amount of water until tender. Drain, mash and set aside.

1 cup flour
1 tablespoon sugar
2 teaspoons baking powder
1 egg
1/2 teaspoon salt
1/2 cup milk
6 tablespoons melted butter or bacon drippings

Mix all ingredients as for pancakes, then add mashed eggplant. Cook on well greased griddle, until very brown, on both sides, adding bacon drippings to griddle after cooking. *Serve hot as fritters or for breakfast with syrup and butter.*

Mashed Turnips

3 cups turnips, pared and diced
Pinch of salt
3 tablespoons real butter
1-1/2 tablespoon sugar
1-1/2 tablespoons half-and-half
Salt and pepper to taste

Boil diced turnips in lightly salted water until tender. Drain well. Mash turnips and stir in butter and sugar. Slowly stir in half-and-half to make a very soft consistence. Add salt and pepper to taste. Serve hot.

Boiled Squash

5-6 squash, cubed
1 cup onions
1/8 cup sugar

Boil squash with onion, drain and slightly mash. Add touch of butter and 1/8 cup sugar. Put back on burner on low to warm, serve hot.

Deviled Beets

2 tablespoon vinegar
1 tablespoon brown sugar
1 tablespoon butter or margarine
1 teaspoon Worcestershire
1/2 teaspoon salt
1/2 teaspoon paprika
1/4 teaspoon dry mustard
1/4 teaspoon cloves
3 cups diced, cooked beets

Combine all ingredients except beets in a medium saucepan; cook, stirring constantly, over low heat about 2 minutes. Stir in beets; cook about 4 minutes. Serves 6.

Herbed Potatoes

1 1/2 pounds new potatoes
3 tablespoon chopped parsley
1/4 cup melted margarine
1 tablespoon chopped fresh chives
1 tablespoon lemon juice

1-1/2 teaspoon chopped fresh dill
Salt and pepper to taste

Pare a 1-inch strip around center of each potato. Cover potatoes and cook in boiling salted water for 25 minutes or until tender. Drain potatoes and set aside. Combine remaining ingredients, stirring well. Pour over potatoes, coating thoroughly. Serves 6.

Stuffed Peppers

3/4 cup quick brown rice (to be cooked)
1-1/2 cup boiling water (to cook rice)
5 large green peppers
1 large onion, finely chopped
1 pound ground lean chuck
2-1/2 cups canned tomatoes
1 teaspoon each - salt, pepper, seasoned salt
2 eggs
2-3 strips of bacon, halved

Cook rice in boiling water for 15 minutes. Cut a thin slice from top of peppers; remove seeds. Drop peppers into boiling water for 3 minutes only. Drain and set upright in baking dish. Mix half the onions, all the beef and half the tomatoes, salt, pepper, seasoned salt; stir in eggs, beaten with a fork.

Mix in cooked rice; pile into peppers. Top each pepper with a piece of bacon. Put rest of tomatoes and chopped onions in dish around peppers. Cover casserole. Bake in hot oven (400 degrees) about 45 minutes. Uncover and bake about 15 minutes to brown on top.

SECTION XIV

Mel's ... Pies

Mel, Jr.

FOOT, FOOT-FOOT, AND ...
FOOT-FOOT-FOOT

Another reason I figure I stutter is, when I was a little boy 'bout 4 years old, my daddy used to tell me a story 'bout some little rabbits. There were three of 'em, and they had little rabbit names. One was named Foot, and one was named Foot-Foot, and one was named Foot-Foot-Foot. They were all brothers and they lived in a fence row next to a once fine garden, but it was gettin' late in the year and all the carrots, turnips and cabbage were gettin' p-p-p-pithy.

So one day, and being the leader of the Foot Brothers, Foot-Foot-Foot said, "Foot and Foot-Foot, I'm Gonna go a-find us a fall garden. This spring garden's 'bout had it. All the carrots and turnips and cabbage are all gettin' p-p-p-pithy. You'all hang tight 'til I get back, and don't eat from the garden."

Foot-Foot-Foot said good-bye to Foot, and Foot said good-bye to Foot-Foot-Foot. Then Foot-Foot-Foot said good-bye to Foot-Foot, and Foot-Foot said good-bye to Foot-Foot-Foot.

Old Foot-Foot-Foot hopped and he hopped and hopped and he hopped and he hopped and he hopped and he hopped. In the meanwhile, ol' Foot got hungry, and going against Foot-Foot-Foot's warning, he ate one of the p-p-p-pithy carrots from the dying garden, and he got sick, too.

Well, he turned orange, the same color of the p-p-p-ithy carrot and he was real bilious.

He was so sick and afraid, that he hopped to Foot-Foot and cried out in agony,

"Foot-Foot!"

"What is it, Foot? You look awful and you're orange, too. What happened?"

Foot said to Foot-Foot,

"Foot-Foot, I'm sick as a dog. I just feel terrible."

Foot-Foot said to Foot,

"Tell me what's happened to you, Foot?"

Foot cried to Foot-Foot," "Foot-Foot, I got real hungry, and I just couldn't hardly stood it, so I went to the dying garden and ate on of the p-p-p-ithy carrots and I think I got carrot poison. Foot-Foot, will you go and find Foot-Foot-Foot and tell him what I've done and tell him that I'm real sick and I think I'm gonna die."

And Foot-Foot said to Foot, "Aw--- Foot, you'll be okay, and Foot-Foot-Foot should be back any day, now."

Foot, not satisfied, said to Foot-Foot," Foot-Foot, please go and tell Foot-Foot-Foot. Another day may be too late."

Finally, Foot-Foot gave in and said, "All right, Foot, if nothing else will please you, I'll go and find Foot-Foot-Foot. In the mean time, you try and get some rest and quit worrying."

Foot-Foot said good-bye to Foot, and Foot said good-bye to Foot-Foot, and then Foot-Foot hopped and he hopped and he hopped and he hopped and he hopped and he hopped and he hopped and he hopped, and after two days hopping, he finally found Foot-Foot-Foot.

Foot-Foot-Foot, surprised, said to Foot-Foot, "Well, hello, Foot-Foot. What's the matter? Is there something wrong? I told you I'd come back to get you'all when I found a fall garden. I'm still looking."

Foot-Foot didn't waste any time in telling Foot-Foot-Foot what had happened to Foot.

"Foot-Foot-Foot, I'm so glad I found you. Foot is real sick. He went against your warning and ate one of thep-p-p-p-pithy carrots from the dying garden, and he thinks he's gonna die. He wants you to come as quickly as you can, Foot-Foot-Foot."

Foot-Foot-Foot said to Foot-Foot, "Foot-Foot, Foot shouldn't have ate the carrot from the dying garden, but none the less, he's not going to die. He may turn a little pale around the gills, but he'll be okay."

"Pale around the gills, Foot-Foot-Foot! Foot has turned completely orange all over, and he wants you to come back."

"Foot-Foot, I'm pretty sure Foot is gonna be all right. You go on back and if he takes a turn for the worse, take him to a po-po-po-dia, po-po-dia, foot doctor."

Foot-Foot said good-bye to Foot-Foot-Foot and Foot-Foot-Foot said good-bye to Foot-Foot, and he hopped and he hopped and he hopped and he hopped and he hopped and he hopped and he hopped and he hopped and finally, got back to where he had left Foot. But, Foot had died.

All four feet were sticking straight up in the air. And it scared old Foot-Foot 'cause he also had a bite off the same carrot.

Foot-Foot wasted no time in getting Foot in the grave. Rabbits get stiff in a hurry, and it is best to inter them right away. Several rabbits who lived close by came to the funeral, and it was a sad day for rabbits. All were affected with grief and sorrow in the passing of Foot, because he was loved by all.

After the funeral, Foot-Foot thanked all the other rabbits for coming and then he hopped and he hopped and he hopped and he hopped and he hopped and he hopped and he hopped and he hopped and he hopped and after two days hopping, he finally found Foot-Foot-Foot and he said,

"Hey, Foot-Foot-Foot!"

Foot-Foot-Foot said, "Hi, Foot-Foot. How's Foot?"

Foot-Foot said to Foot-Foot-Foot,

"Foot-Foot-Foot, Foot's dead. And you know something else, Foot-Foot-Foot, I had a bit off the same bad carrot and I ain't feeling too well. I think I'm gonna die, too."

Foot-Foot-Foot was really shocked when he heard about Foot's passing and he cried out sorrow.

"O-O-O-O-Oh, Foot-Foot. You can't die, too. We've already got *one Foot* in the grave, now!"

PIES

- ◆ Vinegar Pie Crust
- ◆ Key Lime Pie
- ◆ Lemon Chess
- ◆ Sweet Potato Pie
- ◆ Ima's French Blueberry
- ◆ Country Apple Pie
- ◆ Aunt Eula's Pecan Pie
- ◆ Chocolate Pie
- ◆ Fresh Peach Pie
- ◆ Cherry Pie

I've used lots of different recipes for pie crust over the years, but none of 'em tops a Vinegar Pie Crust I ran across 'bout five years ago.

Vinegar Pie Crust

1 teaspoon white vinegar
1 beaten egg
8 tablespoons of Ice Water
1 teaspoon salt
1 cup plus 2 tablespoons of shortenin'
3 cups plain flour.

Blend vinegar and beaten egg; add ice water and salt. Cut shortenin' into flour with pastry blender or do it by hand. Combine the two mixtures into a ball of dough and chill in the refrigerator while you make the fillin'. Yields 3 (9 inch) pie crusts.

Key Lime Pie

6 egg yolks
1 15 ounce can sweetened condensed milk
1/2 cup Key Lime Juice
1 9-inch baked pie shell
6 egg whites, stiffly beaten
4 tablespoons sugar

Combine egg yolks and condensed milk. Mix well. Add lime juice; blend well. Turn into baked pie shell. Beat egg whites until stiff peaks form, gradually adding sugar. Swirl onto pie, spreading to edge of pie shell all around. Bake in 200 degree oven until meringue is pale honey-colored.

Lemon Chess Pie Fillin'

1/4 cup lemon juice
1/4 cup melted butter
1/4 cup Pet Evaporated milk
2 cups sugar
1 tablespoon corn meal
1 tablespoon flour
3 tablespoons grated lemon rind or zest
4 eggs
1 unbaked 9" pie shell

Mix all ingredients together with pour into unbaked pie shell. Start in a cold oven and bake at 325 degrees for 45-60 minutes or until top of pie are golden.

Sweet Potato Pie

1/2 cup (1 stick) margarine
2 cups cooked, mashed sweet potatoes
1-1/2 cups sugar
3 eggs, well beaten
2 teaspoons vanilla
1/4 cup milk
Dash of salt
1/4 teaspoon nutmeg, optional
1 unbaked pie crust (9 inch)

Mash margarine with hot sweet potatoes. Beat in sugar, eggs, vanilla and milk. Add salt to taste if you haven't salted the water in which the potatoes are cooked. Add nutmeg if you want, and stir well. Pour into unbaked pie crust and bake in preheated 350 degree oven 30-40 minutes, or until it won't shake. *Delicious!*

Ima's French Blueberry Pie

2 (3 ounce) packages cream cheese
2 tablespoons milk
1 teaspoon grated lemon peel
1 baked pie shell (9 inch)
1 quart fresh blueberries
t tablespoon lemon juice
1/8 teaspoon salt
Water

1 cup sugar
2 tablespoons cornstarch

Soften cream cheese. Add milk and lemon peel; beat
until smooth. Spread cheese mixture evenly in bottom of
baked pie shell. Sprinkle half (2 cups) of whole blueberries
over cheese layer. Mash remainder of blueberries; spoon into
a 1-1/2 cup measure. Add lemon juice, salt and enough water
to make 1-1/2 cups of pulp and liquid. Place in a small
saucepan. Mix sugar and cornstarch. Stir into the blueberry
pulp. Bring to a boil, stirring constantly, and cook for about 2
minutes or until thickened. Cool mixture to lukewarm.

Spoon the blueberry sauce over blueberries in pie
shell. Chill for several hours. Makes 8 servings.

Apple Pie

Pastry for 9 inch pie crust
7 to 8 medium green apples
1 tablespoon flour
Dash of salt
2/3 to 3/4 cup sugar
1 tablespoon butter
1 tablespoon lemon juice
1/4 teaspoon cinnamon or nutmeg

Prepare pie crust. Roll out bottom crust; line pan and
trim off even with pie rim. Roll out top crust; cut design in
center so the steam can escape. Cover pastry with wax paper
while making your fillin'.

Wash apples, pare, quarter and remove cores, and cut
quarters lengthwise into 3 or 4 slices. There should be a full

quart (4 cups) of sliced apples. Blend flour, salt and sugar; stir 1/4 of mixture over bottom of pastry line pie pan. Stir in the rest, placing the apples close together and piled higher than the rim. Dot with butter, sprinkle with lemon juice and cinnamon.

Moisten the edge of lower pastry with water then place top crust on top of your fillin'. Trim off excess dough around edge, and leave 1/2 overhanging. Press fork tines down around the pie crust on edges firmly.

Bake in hot oven...450 degrees for 15 minutes, then reduce heat to 325 degrees and bake until apples are tender and juice boils through your vents. Remove and cool.

Aunt Eula's Pecan Pie

1 cup pecan halves
Pastry for 9 inch pie crust
3 eggs
1 tablespoon melted butter
1 cup light corn syrup
1/2 teaspoon vanilla
1 cup sugar
1 tablespoon flour

Arrange pecan halves in bottom of pie shell. Beat the eggs, add butter, corn syrup and vanilla. Stir until well mixed. Combine the sugar and flour and blend with egg mixture; pour over nuts in the pie shell. Let stand until the nuts rise to the surface.

Bake in moderate oven (350 degrees) for 45 minutes.
The nuts will glaze while baking.

Chocolate Pie

1/2 cup butter
3/4 cup sugar
1 ounce chocolate
1 teaspoon vanilla
2 eggs
1 baked 8" pie shell
Whipped cream

Cream butter, add sugar gradually, blend in the
chocolate, melted and cooled. Add vanilla. Add one egg at a
time, beating after each addition. Turn into baked 8" pie shell;
chill 2 hours or more. Serve with whipped cream.

Fresh Peach Pie

Pastry for 9 inch pie
4 cups sliced peaches
1 cup sugar (or 1/2 brown sugar and 1/2 granulated)
1/4 teaspoon salt
1 tablespoon flour
2 tablespoons butter or margarine

Fill pastry lined pie pan with sliced peaches and cover
em' with sugar, salt and flour. Dot with butter. Top with
lattice strips if you want. Bake in very hot oven (450 degrees)
10 minutes. Reduce heat to 350 degrees and bake about 30
minutes longer.

Fresh Cherry Pie

1 cup sugar (1-1/4 for sour cherries)
1/4 teaspoon salt
2 tablespoons cornstarch or 2 1/2 tablespoons
      Tapioca
1 quart cherries, pitted
Pastry for double crust 9 inch pie
2 tablespoons butter or margarine
Milk or cream (optional)

Combine sugar, salt and cornstarch. Add to the pitted cherries. Place fruit in pie pan. Dot with butter. Cover to with top crust, slashed to allow steam to escape. If you want a glaze, brush top with milk or cream. Bake in very hot oven (425 degrees) for 15 minutes, reduce to 350 degrees and bake 30 minutes longer.

SECTION XV

Mel's ... Cakes

"Too much salt in the icing, dad!" (Cindy, Pam, and Connie)

CAKES

◆ Sweet Chocolate Cake
◆ Mel's Pumpkin Cheesecake
◆ Mama's Fruit Cake
◆ Daddy's Spice Cake
◆ Orange Coconut Cake
◆ Strawberry Cake
◆ Orange Flavored Holiday Cake
◆ Red Devil's Cake
◆ Old Style Pound Cake
◆ Mayonnaise Cake

Sweet Chocolate Cake

1 package sweet cooking chocolate
1/2 cup boiling water
1 cup butter, margarine or other shortenin'
2 cups sugar
4 egg yolks, unbeaten
1 teaspoon vanilla
2-1/2 cups sifted cake flour
1 teaspoon baking soda
1/2 teaspoon salt
1 cup buttermilk
4 egg whites, stiffly beaten

Melt chocolate in 1/2 cup boiling water. Cool. Cream butter and sugar until light and fluffy. Add egg yolks one at a time, beating after each. Add vanilla and melted chocolate and mix until well blended. Sift flour with soda and salt.

Add sifted dry ingredients alternately with buttermilk, beating after each addition until batter is smooth. Fold in

160

stiffly beaten egg whites. Pour batter into three 8 or 9" layer pans lined on bottom with paper. Bake at 350 degrees for 35 to 40 minutes. Cool. Frost top and between layers with Coconut Pecan Filling and Frosting.

Coconut Pecan Filling and Frosting:

1 cup evaporated milk
1 cup sugar
3 egg yolks
1/4 pound butter or margarine
1 teaspoon vanilla
1-3/4 cups flaked coconut
1 cup chopped pecans

Combine milk, sugar, egg yolks, butter and vanilla in saucepan. Cook over medium heat, stirring constantly, until mixture thickens, about 12 minutes. Remove from heat. Add coconut and pecans, beat until cool and of spreading consistency.

Mel's Pumpkin Cheesecake

Nut Crust:

2 cups ground pecans
2 tablespoons brown sugar
1 egg white, beaten until frothy
1 teaspoon powdered ginger
1 teaspoon finely grated lemon rind

Mix pecans with brown sugar, egg white, powdered ginger and rind just until mixture is bound together. Press into the bottom and a little up the sides of a 10-inch springform pan.

Filling:

2-1/2 pounds cream cheese, softened
1 cup granulated sugar
4 large eggs, lightly beaten
3 egg yolks, lightly beaten
3 tablespoons flour
2 teaspoons ground cinnamon
1 teaspoon ground cloves
1 teaspoon ground ginger
2 teaspoons finely grated lemon rind
1 cup heavy cream
1 tablespoon vanilla extract
1 pound can pumpkin puree
Coarsely grated lemon rind for garnish

Beat together cream cheese, sugar, eggs and yolks.
Add flour, cinnamon, cloves, ginger and lemon rind. Beat in
cream and vanilla; add pumpkin and beat until thoroughly
mixed. Pour into prepared crust and bake 15 minutes at 425
degrees. Reduce heat to 275 degrees and bake 1 hour longer.
Turn off heat and allow cake to cool overnight or for 8 hours
in the oven. Refrigerate for several hours or overnight before
serving.

Mama's Fruitcake

1 pound butter
1 pound brown sugar
4 egg yolks
1 teaspoon nutmeg
1/2 teaspoon cinnamon
1/2 teaspoon allspice
1 pound flour
1 cup milk
4 egg whites

5 pounds candied fruit
1 to 2 pounds chopped nuts, as desired

Cream butter and sugar, add egg yolks, add spices, then flour and milk alternately. Fold in egg whites which have been beaten 'til stiff. Add this mixture to the fruit and nuts, which have been cut into small pieces and rubbed with additional flour to prevent sticking.

Pour into several cake tins which have been lined with 4 thicknesses of waxed paper. Bake in a slow oven (250 degrees) for 3 hours, or when cake tester comes out clean. This recipe makes 12 to 15 pound cake, depending on the amount of nuts added. It makes one large and one small tube pan cake, and several loaves. Bake in October, wrap in foil and store in tight container to age.

Daddy's Spice Cake

1/2 cup shortenin'
1/2 cup brown sugar, packed
1/2 cup granulated sugar
2 eggs
1/2 teaspoon baking soda
1/4 teaspoon salt
1 teaspoon cinnamon
1/4 teaspoon nutmeg
2 cups sifted cake flour
1/2 teaspoon allspice
2 teaspoons baking powder
1/2 teaspoon cloves
1 cup beer

Cream shortenin', add sugars gradually, blending thoroughly. Add eggs, beat thoroughly. Mix and sift dry ingredients. Add to creamed mixture alternately with beer, beginning and ending with dry ingredients. Turn into greased 8x8x2" pan. Bake in moderate oven, 40-45 minutes.

Orange Coconut Cake

3/4 cup Crisco shortening
3/4 teaspoon salt
Grated rind of 1 orange
1-1/2 cups sugar
3 eggs, unbeaten
3 cups sifted cake flour
3 teaspoons baking powder
Juice of 1 orange
2 tablespoons lemon juice
1 cup shredded coconut

Combine Crisco, salt, grated orange rind; add sugar gradually and cream until light and fluffy. Add eggs, one at a time; beat thoroughly after each addition. Sift the flour and baking powder together 3 times.

Combine orange juice and lemon juice and add water to make 1 cup. Add a small amount of flour to creamed mixture, alternately with combined fruit juice and water, beating after each addition until smooth. Pour batter into four 9" layer pans greased with Crisco. Bake in moderately hot oven (350 degrees) for 40-45 minutes. Also can be used in a large pan.

Frosting:

1-1/2 cup sugar
1/2 teaspoon light corn syrup
1/2 cup boiling water

2 egg whites, stiffly beaten
1 teaspoon vanilla

Combine sugar, corn syrup and boiling water in saucepan and cook until mixture spins a long thread. Pour syrup slowly over beaten egg whites, beating constantly; add vanilla and beat until frosting is cool and stiff enough to hold its shape. Makes enough frosting to cover tops and sides of two 9" layers.

Strawberry Cake

1 box white cake mix
1 box strawberry gelatin
2/3 cup salad oil (or soft butter)
4 eggs
1 cup frozen strawberries, thawed

Sift dry white cake mix and gelatin powder together. Blend in oil (or soft butter). Add eggs one at a time, beating with each addition. Add the thawed strawberries. Turn into two 9" pans, greased and floured, and bake 30 minutes, or until done, at 350 degrees. Frost and fill with icing made of:

1 box sifted confectioners sugar
1 stick melted butter
Blend and add 1/2 cup thawed strawberries

Orange Flavored Holiday Cake

1 cup butter
2 cups granulated sugar
4 whole eggs
3 cups cake flour

3 teaspoons baking powder
1/4 teaspoon salt
1 cup orange juice

Cream butter and sugar, add 1 egg at a time; sift flour then measure, add baking powder and alt and sift three times and add to first mixture alternately with orange juice. Pour into two 9" pans, greased and floured.

Bake at 375 degrees for 35 minutes. Cool and spread orange filling between layers and top.

Orange Filling:

1-1/2 cups granulated sugar
6 teaspoons all purpose flour
1 teaspoon grated orange rind
1 cup hot water
2 egg yolks
2 teaspoons lemon juice
1 cup orange juice
1 teaspoon butter
1 cup coconut

Mix sugar, flour and grated rind together, adding hot water slowly. Add 2 well beaten egg yolks, cook in double boiler until it begins to thicken.

Add lemon and orange juices and continue cooking for about 20 minutes. Remove from the heat; add butter and coconut. Cool and spread on cake. Frost sides with marshmallow icing.

Red Devil's Food Cake

1 cup butter
2 cups sugar
1/2 teaspoon salt
1/2 cup cocoa
5 eggs, separated
2-1/2 cups sifted cake flour
1 cup buttermilk
1 teaspoon vanilla
1 teaspoon soda in 1 tablespoon boiling water
1 teaspoon red food coloring

Cream together butter and sugar, add salt, cocoa and beaten egg yolks. Alternately add flour and buttermilk, mix well. Add vanilla, food coloring, and then soda dissolved in boiling water. Lastly fold in beaten egg whites. Bake in 9" layer cake pans in moderate oven (350 degrees) for 40-45 minutes.

Chocolate Frosting:

1/3 cup butter
1 pound confectioners sugar, sifted
4 tablespoons cream
1-1/2 teaspoon vanilla
3 squares melted unsweetened chocolate

Cream butter and add sifted sugar alternately with cream. Add vanilla and melted unsweetened chocolate. Blend thoroughly and spread on cake.

Old Style Pound Cake

2 cups sifted flour
½ teaspoon baking powder
1/4 teaspoon salt
1 cup butter
1-1/2 cups sugar
5 eggs
2 tablespoons lemon juice

Heat oven to 325 degrees. Grease bottom of loaf pan and lightly flour. Sift together flour, baking powder and salt. Cream butter and gradually add sugar, beating all the time. Beat in eggs, one at a time. Add flour mixture. Add lemon juice. Put batter in greased ban and bake about 1 hour and 10 minutes. *Perfect with a glass of cold milk!*

Mayonnaise Cake

1 package (17-1/2 ounce) Fudge Cake mix
1-1/2 cups water
2 eggs
1/2 cup mayonnaise

Generously grease and lightly flour 13x9 inch pan. In large mixing bowl, combine cake mix, water, eggs and mayonnaise. Blend and beat as directed on package. Pour into prepared pan. Bake at 350 degrees for 20-35 minutes, until toothpick inserted in center comes out clean. Frost.

Recipe Index

169

PANTRY BASICS

A WELL-STOCKED PANTRY provides all the makings for a good meal. With the right ingredients, you can quickly create a variety of satisfying, delicious meals for family or guests. Keeping these items in stock also means avoiding extra trips to the grocery store, saving you time and money. Although everyone's pantry is different, there are basic items you should always have. Add other items according to your family's needs. For example, while some families consider chips, cereals and snacks as must-haves, others can't be without feta cheese and imported olives. Use these basic pantry suggestions as a handy reference list when creating your grocery list. Don't forget refrigerated items like milk, eggs, cheese and butter.

STAPLES

Baker's chocolate
Baking powder
Baking soda
Barbeque sauce
Bread crumbs (plain or seasoned)
Chocolate chips
Cocoa powder
Cornmeal
Cornstarch
Crackers
Flour
Honey
Ketchup
Lemon juice
Mayonnaise or salad dressing
Non-stick cooking spray
Nuts (almonds, pecans, walnuts)
Oatmeal
Oil (olive, vegetable)
Pancake baking mix
Pancake syrup
Peanut butter
Shortening
Sugar (granulated, brown, powdered)
Vinegar

PACKAGED/CANNED FOODS

Beans (canned, dry)
Broth (beef, chicken)
Cake mixes with frosting
Canned diced tomatoes
Canned fruit
Canned mushrooms
Canned soup
Canned tomato paste & sauce
Canned tuna & chicken
Cereal
Dried soup mix
Gelatin (flavored or plain)
Gravies
Jarred Salsa
Milk (evaporated, sweetened condensed)
Non-fat dry milk
Pastas
Rice (brown, white)
Spaghetti sauce

SPICES/SEASONINGS

Basil
Bay leaves
Black pepper
Boullion cubes (beef, chicken)
Chives
Chili powder
Cinnamon
Mustard (dried, prepared)
Garlic powder or salt
Ginger
Nutmeg
Onion powder or salt
Oregano
Paprika
Parsley
Rosemary
Sage
Salt
Soy sauce
Tarragon
Thyme
Vanilla
Worcestershire sauce
Yeast

HERBS & SPICES

DRIED VS. FRESH. While dried herbs are convenient, they don't generally have the same purity of flavor as fresh herbs. Ensure dried herbs are still fresh by checking if they are green and not faded. Crush a few leaves to see if the aroma is still strong. Always store them in an air-tight container away from light and heat.

BASIL
Sweet, warm flavor with an aromatic odor. Use whole or ground. Good with lamb, fish, roast, stews, beef, vegetables, dressing and omelets.

BAY LEAVES
Pungent flavor. Use whole leaf but remove before serving. Good in vegetable dishes, seafood, stews and pickles.

CARAWAY
Spicy taste and aromatic smell. Use in cakes, breads, soups, cheese and sauerkraut.

CELERY SEED
Strong taste which resembles the vegetable. Can be used sparingly in pickles and chutney, meat and fish dishes, salads, bread, marinades, dressings and dips.

CHIVES
Sweet, mild flavor like that of onion. Excellent in salads, fish, soups and potatoes.

CILANTRO
Use fresh. Excellent in salads, fish, chicken, rice, beans and Mexican dishes.

CINNAMON
Sweet, pungent flavor. Widely used in many sweet baked goods, chocolate dishes, cheesecakes, pickles, chutneys and hot drinks.

CORIANDER
Mild, sweet, orangy flavor and available whole or ground. Common in curry powders and pickling spice and also used in chutney, meat dishes, casseroles, Greek-style dishes, apple pies and baked goods.

CURRY POWDER
Spices are combined to proper proportions to give a distinct flavor to meat, poultry, fish and vegetables.

DILL
Both seeds and leaves are flavorful. Leaves may be used as a garnish or cooked with fish, soup, dressings, potatoes and beans. Leaves or the whole plant may be used to flavor pickles.

FENNEL
Sweet, hot flavor. Both seeds and leaves are used. Use in small quantities in pies and baked goods. Leaves can be boiled with fish.

HERBS & SPICES

GINGER
A pungent root, this aromatic spice is sold fresh, dried or ground. Use in pickles, preserves, cakes, cookies, soups and meat dishes.

MARJORAM
May be used both dried or green. Use to flavor fish, poultry, omelets, lamb, stew, stuffing and tomato juice.

MINT
Aromatic with a cool flavor. Excellent in beverages, fish, lamb, cheese, soup, peas, carrots and fruit desserts.

NUTMEG
Whole or ground. Used in chicken and cream soups, cheese dishes, fish cakes, and with chicken and veal. Excellent in custards, milk puddings, pies and cakes.

OREGANO
Strong, aromatic odor. Use whole or ground in tomato juice, fish, eggs, pizza, omelets, chili, stew, gravy, poultry and vegetables.

PAPRIKA
A bright red pepper, this spice is used in meat, vegetables and soups or as a garnish for potatoes, salads or eggs.

PARSLEY
Best when used fresh, but can be used dried as a garnish or as a seasoning. Try in fish, omelets, soup, meat, stuffing and mixed greens.

ROSEMARY
Very aromatic. Can be used fresh or dried. Season fish, stuffing, beef, lamb, poultry, onions, eggs, bread and potatoes. Great in dressings.

SAFFRON
Aromatic, slightly bitter taste. Only a pinch needed to flavor and color dishes such as bouillabaisse, chicken soup, rice, paella, fish sauces, buns and cakes. Very expensive, so where a touch of color is needed, use turmeric instead, but the flavor will not be the same.

SAGE
Use fresh or dried. The flowers are sometimes used in salads. May be used in tomato juice, fish, omelets, beef, poultry, stuffing, cheese spreads and breads.

TARRAGON
Leaves have a pungent, hot taste. Use to flavor sauces, salads, fish, poultry, tomatoes, eggs, green beans, carrots and dressings.

THYME
Sprinkle leaves on fish or poultry before broiling or baking. Throw a few sprigs directly on coals shortly before meat is finished grilling.

TURMERIC
Aromatic, slightly bitter flavor. Should be used sparingly in curry powder and relishes and to color cakes and rice dishes.

**Use 3 times more fresh herbs
if substituting fresh for dried.**

HINTS FOR BAKING BREADS

• Kneading dough for 30 seconds after mixing improves the texture of baking powder biscuits.

• Instead of shortening, use cooking or salad oil in waffles and hot cakes.

• When bread is baking, a small dish of water in the oven will help keep the crust from hardening.

• Dip a spoon in hot water to measure shortening, butter, etc., and the fat will slip out more easily.

• Small amounts of leftover corn may be added to pancake batter for variety.

• To make bread crumbs, use the fine cutter of a food grinder and tie a large paper bag over the spout in order to prevent flying crumbs.

• When you are doing any sort of baking, you get better results if you remember to preheat your cookie sheet, muffin tins or cake pans.

3 RULES FOR USE OF LEAVENING AGENTS

1. In simple flour mixtures, use 2 teaspoons baking powder to leaven 1 cup flour. Reduce this amount 1/2 teaspoon for each egg used.

2. To 1 teaspoon soda, use 2 1/4 teaspoons cream of tartar, 2 cups freshly soured milk or 1 cup molasses.

3. To substitute soda and an acid for baking powder, divide the amount of baking powder by 4. Take that as your measure and add acid according to rule 2.

PROPORTIONS OF BAKING POWDER TO FLOUR

biscuits ....to 1 cup flour use 1 1/4 tsp. baking powder
cake with oil ....to 1 cup flour use 1 tsp. baking powder
muffins ....to 1 cup flour use 1 1/2 tsp. baking powder
popovers ....to 1 cup flour use 1 1/4 tsp. baking powder
waffles ....to 1 cup flour use 1 1/4 tsp. baking powder

PROPORTIONS OF LIQUID TO FLOUR

pour batter ....to 1 cup liquid use 1 cup flour
drop batter ....to 1 cup liquid use 2 to 2 1/2 cups flour
soft dough ....to 1 cup liquid use 3 to 3 1/2 cups flour
stiff dough ....to 1 cup liquid use 4 cups flour

TIME & TEMPERATURE CHART

Breads	Minutes	Temperature
biscuits	12 - 15	400° - 450°
cornbread	25 - 30	400° - 425°
gingerbread	40 - 50	350° - 370°
loaf	50 - 60	350° - 400°
nut bread	50 - 75	350°
popovers	30 - 40	425° - 450°
rolls	20 - 30	400° - 450°

BAKING DESSERTS

PERFECT COOKIES

Cookie dough that must be rolled is much easier to handle after it has been refrigerated for 10 to 30 minutes. This keeps the dough from sticking, even though it may be soft. If not done, the soft dough may require more flour and too much flour makes cookies hard and brittle. Place on a floured board only as much dough as can be easily managed. Flour the rolling pin slightly and roll lightly to desired thickness. Cut shapes close together and add trimmings to dough that needs to be rolled. Place pans or sheets in upper third of oven. Watch cookies carefully while baking in order to avoid burned edges. When sprinkling sugar on cookies, try putting it into a salt shaker in order to save time.

PERFECT PIES

• Pie crust will be better and easier to make if all the ingredients are cool.

• The lower crust should be placed in the pan so that it covers the surface smoothly. Air pockets beneath the surface will push the crust out of shape while baking.

• Folding the top crust over the lower crust before crimping will keep juices in the pie.

• When making custard pie, bake at a high temperature for about 10 minutes to prevent a soggy crust. Then finish baking at a low temperature.

• When making cream pie, sprinkle crust with powdered sugar in order to prevent it from becoming soggy.

PERFECT CAKES

• Fill cake pans two-thirds full and spread batter into corners and sides, leaving a slight hollow in the center.

• Cake is done when it shrinks from the sides of the pan or if it springs back when touched lightly with the finger.

• After removing a cake from the oven, place it on a rack for about 5 minutes. Then, the sides should be loosened and the cake turned out on a rack in order to finish cooling.

• Do not frost cakes until thoroughly cool.

• Icing will remain where you put it if you sprinkle cake with powdered sugar first.

TIME & TEMPERATURE CHART

Dessert	Time	Temperature
butter cake, layer	20-40 min.	380° - 400°
butter cake, loaf	40-60 min.	360° - 400°
cake, angel	50-60 min.	300° - 360°
cake, fruit	3-4 hrs.	275° - 325°
cake, sponge	40-60 min.	300° - 350°
cookies, molasses	18-20 min.	350° - 375°
cookies, thin	10-12 min.	380° - 390°
cream puffs	45-60 min.	300° - 350°
meringue	40-60 min.	250° - 300°
pie crust	20-40 min.	400° - 500°

VEGETABLES & FRUITS

COOKING TIME TABLE

Vegetable	Cooking Method	Time
artichokes	boiled	40 min.
	steamed	45-60 min.
asparagus tips	boiled	10-15 min.
beans, lima	boiled	20-40 min.
	steamed	60 min.
beans, string	boiled	15-35 min.
	steamed	60 min.
beets, old	boiled or steamed	1-2 hours.
beets, young with skin	boiled	30 min.
	steamed	60 min.
	baked	70-90 min.
broccoli, flowerets	boiled	5-10 min.
broccoli, stems	boiled	20-30 min.
brussels sprouts	boiled	20-30 min.
cabbage, chopped	boiled	10-20 min.
	steamed	25 min.
carrots, cut across	boiled	8-10 min.
	steamed	40 min.
cauliflower, flowerets	boiled	8-10 min.
cauliflower, stem down	boiled	20-30 min.
corn, green, tender	boiled	5-10 min.
	steamed	15 min.
	baked	20 min.
corn on the cob	boiled	8-10 min.
	steamed	15 min.
eggplant, whole	boiled	30 min.
	steamed	40 min.
	baked	45 min.
parsnips	boiled	25-40 min.
	steamed	60 min.
	baked	60-75 min.
peas, green	boiled or steamed	5-15 min.
potatoes	boiled	20-40 min.
	steamed	60 min.
	baked	45-60 min.
pumpkin or squash	boiled	20-40 min.
	steamed	45 min.
	baked	60 min.
tomatoes	boiled	5-15 min.
turnips	boiled	25-40 min.

DRYING TIME TABLE

Fruit	Sugar or Honey	Cooking Time
apricots	1/4 c. for each cup of fruit	about 40 min.
figs	1 T. for each cup of fruit	about 30 min.
peaches	1/4 c. for each cup of fruit	about 45 min.
prunes	2 T. for each cup of fruit	about 45 min.

VEGETABLES & FRUITS

BUYING FRESH VEGETABLES

Artichokes: Look for compact, tightly closed heads with green, clean-looking leaves. Avoid those with leaves that are brown or separated.

Asparagus: Stalks should be tender and firm; tips should be close and compact. Choose the stalks with very little white; they are more tender. Use asparagus soon because it toughens quickly.

Beans, Snap: Those with small seeds inside the pods are best. Avoid beans with dry-looking pods.

Broccoli, Brussels Sprouts and Cauliflower: Flower clusters on broccoli and cauliflower should be tight and close together. Brussels sprouts should be firm and compact. Smudgy, dirty spots may indicate pests or disease.

Cabbage and Head Lettuce: Choose heads that are heavy for their size. Avoid cabbage with worm holes and lettuce with discoloration or soft rot.

Cucumbers: Choose long, slender cucumbers for best quality. May be dark or medium green, but yellow ones are undesirable.

Mushrooms: Caps should be closed around the stems. Avoid black or brown gills.

Peas and Lima Beans: Select pods that are well-filled but not bulging. Avoid dried, spotted, yellow or limp pods.

BUYING FRESH FRUITS

Bananas: Skin should be free of bruises and black or brown spots. Purchase them slightly green and allow them to ripen at room temperature.

Berries: Select plump, solid berries with good color. Avoid stained containers which indicate wet or leaky berries. Berries with clinging caps, such as blackberries and raspberries, may be unripe. Strawberries without caps may be overripe.

Melons: In cantaloupes, thick, close netting on the rind indicates best quality. Cantaloupes are ripe when the stem scar is smooth and the space between the netting is yellow or yellow-green. They are best when fully ripe with fruity odor.

Honeydews are ripe when rind has creamy to yellowish color and velvety texture. Immature honeydews are whitish-green.

Ripe watermelons have some yellow color on one side. If melons are white or pale green on one side, they are not ripe.

Oranges, Grapefruit and Lemons: Choose those heavy for their size. Smoother, thinner skins usually indicate more juice. Most skin markings do not affect quality. Oranges with a slight greenish tinge may be just as ripe as fully colored ones. Light or greenish-yellow lemons are more tart than deep yellow ones. Avoid citrus fruits showing withered, sunken or soft areas.

NAPKIN FOLDING

FOR BEST RESULTS, use well-starched linen napkins if possible. For more complicated folds, 24-inch napkins work best. Practice the folds with newspapers. Children will have fun decorating the table once they learn these attractive folds!

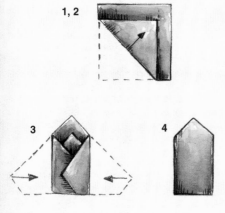

SHIELD

Easy fold. Elegant with monogram in corner.

Instructions:
1. Fold into quarter size. If monogrammed, ornate corner should face down.
2. Turn up folded corner three-quarters.
3. Overlap right side and left side points.
4. Turn over; adjust sides so they are even, single point in center.
5. Place point up or down on plate, or left of plate.

ROSETTE

Elegant on plate.

Instructions:
1. Fold left and right edges to center, leaving 1/2" opening along center.
2. Pleat firmly from top edge to bottom edge. Sharpen edges with hot iron.
3. Pinch center together. If necessary, use small piece of pipe cleaner to secure and top with single flower.
4. Spread out rosette.

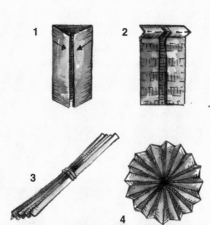

NAPKIN FOLDING

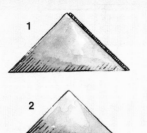

CANDLE

Easy to do; can be decorated.

Instructions:
1. Fold into triangle, point at top.
2. Turn lower edge up 1".
3. Turn over, folded edge down.
4. Roll tightly from left to right.
5. Tuck in corner. Stand upright.

FAN

Pretty in napkin ring or on plate.

Instructions:
1. Fold top and bottom edges to center.
2. Fold top and bottom edges to center a second time.
3. Pleat firmly from the left edge. Sharpen edges with hot iron.
4. Spread out fan. Balance flat folds of each side on table. Well-starched napkins will hold shape.

LILY

Effective and pretty on table.

Instructions:
1. Fold napkin into quarters.
2. Fold into triangle, closed corner to open points.
3. Turn two points over to other side. (Two points are on either side of closed point.)
4. Pleat.
5. Place closed end in glass. Pull down two points on each side and shape.

MEASUREMENTS & SUBSTITUTIONS

MEASUREMENTS

a pinch	1/8 teaspoon or less
3 teaspoons	1 tablespoon
4 tablespoons	1/4 cup
8 tablespoons	1/2 cup
12 tablespoons	3/4 cup
16 tablespoons	1 cup
2 cups	1 pint
4 cups	1 quart
4 quarts	1 gallon
8 quarts	1 peck
4 pecks	1 bushel
16 ounces	1 pound
32 ounces	1 quart
1 ounce liquid	2 tablespoons
8 ounces liquid	1 cup

Use standard measuring spoons and cups. All measurements are level.

C° TO F° CONVERSION

120° C	250° F
140° C	275° F
150° C	300° F
160° C	325° F
180° C	350° F
190° C	375° F
200° C	400° F
220° C	425° F
230° C	450° F

Temperature conversions are estimates.

SUBSTITUTIONS

Ingredient	Quantity	Substitute
baking powder	1 teaspoon	1/4 tsp. baking soda plus 1/2 tsp. cream of tartar
chocolate	1 square (1 oz.)	3 or 4 T. cocoa plus 1 T. butter
cornstarch	1 tablespoon	2 T. flour or 2 tsp. quick-cooking tapioca
cracker crumbs	3/4 cup	1 c. bread crumbs
dates	1 lb.	1 1/2 c. dates, pitted and cut
dry mustard	1 teaspoon	1 T. prepared mustard
flour, self-rising	1 cup	1 c. all-purpose flour, 1/2 tsp. salt, and 1 tsp. baking powder
herbs, fresh	1 tablespoon	1 tsp. dried herbs
ketchup or chili sauce	1 cup	1 c. tomato sauce plus 1/2 c. sugar and 2 T. vinegar (for use in cooking)
milk, sour	1 cup	1 T. lemon juice or vinegar plus sweet milk to make 1 c. (let stand 5 minutes)
whole	1 cup	1/2 c. evaporated milk plus 1/2 c. water
min. marshmallows	10	1 lg. marshmallow
onion, fresh	1 small	1 T. instant minced onion, rehydrated
sugar, brown	1/2 cup	2 T. molasses in 1/2 c. granulated sugar
powdered	1 cup	1 c. granulated sugar plus 1 tsp. cornstarch
tomato juice	1 cup	1/2 c. tomato sauce plus 1/2 c. water

When substituting cocoa for chocolate in cakes, the amount of flour must be reduced. Brown and white sugars usually can be interchanged.

SUGAR

EQUIVALENCY CHART

Food	Quantity	Yield
apple	1 medium	1 cup
banana, mashed	1 medium	1/3 cup
bread	1 1/2 slices	1 cup soft crumbs
bread	1 slice	1/4 cup fine, dry crumbs
butter	1 stick or 1/4 pound	1/2 cup
cheese, American, cubed	1 pound	2 2/3 cups
American, grated	1 pound	5 cups
cream cheese	3-ounce package	6 2/3 tablespoons
chocolate, bitter	1 square	1 ounce
cocoa	1 pound	4 cups
coconut	1 1/2 pound package	2 2/3 cups
coffee, ground	1 pound	5 cups
cornmeal	1 pound	3 cups
cornstarch	1 pound	3 cups
crackers, graham	14 squares	1 cup fine crumbs
saltine	28 crackers	1 cup fine crumbs
egg	4-5 whole	1 cup
whites	8-10	1 cup
yolks	10-12	1 cup
evaporated milk	1 cup	3 cups whipped
flour, cake, sifted	1 pound	4 1/2 cups
rye	1 pound	5 cups
white, sifted	1 pound	4 cups
white, unsifted	1 pound	3 3/4 cups
gelatin, flavored	3 1/4 ounces	1/2 cup
unflavored	1/4 ounce	1 tablespoon
lemon	1 medium	3 tablespoon juice
marshmallows	16	1/4 pound
noodles, cooked	8-ounce package	7 cups
uncooked	4 ounces (1 1/2 cups)	2-3 cups cooked
macaroni, cooked	8-ounce package	6 cups
macaroni, uncooked	4 ounces (1 1/4 cups)	2 1/4 cups cooked
spaghetti, uncooked	7 ounces	4 cups cooked
nuts, chopped	1/4 pound	1 cup
almonds	1 pound	3 1/2 cups
walnuts, broken	1 pound	3 cups
walnuts, unshelled	1 pound	1 1/2 to 1 3/4 cups
onion	1 medium	1/2 cup
orange	3-4 medium	1 cup juice
raisins	1 pound	3 1/2 cups
rice, brown	1 cup	4 cups cooked
converted	1 cup	3 1/2 cups cooked
regular	1 cup	3 cups cooked
wild	1 cup	4 cups cooked
sugar, brown	1 pound	2 1/2 cups
powdered	1 pound	3 1/2 cups
white	1 pound	2 cups
vanilla wafers	22	1 cup fine crumbs
zwieback, crumbled	4	1 cups

FOOD QUANTITIES

FOR LARGE SERVINGS

	25 Servings	50 Servings	100 Servings
Beverages:			
coffee	½ pound and 1 ½ gallons water	1 pound and 3 gallons water	2 pounds and 6 gallons water
lemonade	10-15 lemons and 1 ½ gallons water	20-30 lemons and 3 gallons water	40-60 lemons and 6 gallons water
tea	1/12 pound and 1 ½ gallons water	1/6 pound and 3 gallons water	1/3 pound and 6 gallons water
Desserts:			
layered cake	1 12" cake	3 10" cakes	6 10" cakes
sheet cake	1 10" x 12" cake	1 12" x 20" cake	2 12" x 20" cakes
watermelon	37 ½ pounds	75 pounds	150 pounds
whipping cream	¾ pint	1 ½ to 2 pints	3-4 pints
Ice cream:			
brick	3 ¼ quarts	6 ½ quarts	13 quarts
bulk	2 ¼ quarts	4 ½ quarts or 1 ¼ gallons	9 quarts or 2 ½ gallons
Meat, poultry or fish:			
fish	13 pounds	25 pounds	50 pounds
fish, fillets or steak	7 ½ pounds	15 pounds	30 pounds
hamburger	9 pounds	18 pounds	35 pounds
turkey or chicken	13 pounds	25 to 35 pounds	50 to 75 pounds
wieners (beef)	6 ½ pounds	13 pounds	25 pounds
Salads, casseroles:			
baked beans	¾ gallon	1 ¼ gallons	2 ½ gallons
jello salad	¾ gallon	1 ¼ gallons	2 ½ gallons
potato salad	4 ¼ quarts	2 ¼ gallons	4 ½ gallons
scalloped potatoes	4 ½ quarts or 1 12" x 20" pan	9 quarts or 2 ¼ gallons	18 quarts 4 ½ gallons
spaghetti	1 ¼ gallons	2 ½ gallons	5 gallons
Sandwiches:			
bread	50 slices or 3 1-pound loaves	100 slices or 6 1-pound loaves	200 slices or 12 1-pound loaves
butter	½ pound	1 pound	2 pounds
lettuce	1 ½ heads	3 heads	6 heads
mayonnaise	1 cup	2 cups	4 cups
mixed filling			
meat, eggs, fish	1 ½ quarts	3 quarts	6 quarts
jam, jelly	1 quart	2 quarts	4 quarts

QUICK FIXES

PRACTICALLY EVERYONE has experienced that dreadful moment in the kitchen when a recipe failed and dinner guests have arrived. Perhaps a failed timer, distraction or a missing or mismeasured ingredient is to blame. These handy tips can save the day!

Acidic foods – Sometimes a tomato-based sauce will become too acidic. Add baking soda, one teaspoon at a time, to the sauce. Use sugar as a sweeter alternative.

Burnt food on pots and pans – Allow the pan to cool on its own. Remove as much of the food as possible. Fill with hot water and add a capful of liquid fabric softener to the pot; let it stand for a few hours. You'll have an easier time removing the burnt food.

Chocolate seizes – Chocolate can seize (turn course and grainy) when it comes into contact with water. Place seized chocolate in a metal bowl over a large saucepan with an inch of simmering water in it. Over medium heat, slowly whisk in warm heavy cream. Use 1/4 cup cream to 4 ounces of chocolate. The chocolate will melt and become smooth.

Forgot to thaw whipped topping – Thaw in microwave for 1 minute on the defrost setting. Stir to blend well. Do not over thaw!

Hands smell like garlic or onion – Rinse hands under cold water while rubbing them with a large stainless steel spoon.

Hard brown sugar – Place in a paper bag and microwave for a few seconds, or place hard chunks in a food processor.

Jello too hard – Heat on a low microwave power setting for a very short time.

Lumpy gravy or sauce – Use a blender, food processor or simply strain.

No tomato juice – Mix 1/2 cup ketchup with 1/2 cup water.

Out of honey – Substitute 1 1/4 cups sugar dissolved in 1 cup water.

Overcooked sweet potatoes or carrots – Softened sweet potatoes and carrots make a wonderful soufflé with the addition of eggs and sugar. Consult your favorite cookbook for a good soufflé recipe. Overcooked sweet potatoes can also be used as pie filling.

Sandwich bread is stale – Toast or microwave bread briefly. Otherwise, turn it into breadcrumbs. Bread exposed to light and heat will hasten its demise, so consider using a bread box.

Soup, sauce, gravy too thin – Add 1 tablespoon of flour to hot soup, sauce or gravy. Whisk well (to avoid lumps) while the mixture is boiling. Repeat if necessary.

Sticky rice – Rinse rice with warm water.

Stew or soup is greasy – Refrigerate and remove grease once it congeals. Another trick is to lay cold lettuce leaves over the hot stew for about 10 seconds and then remove. Repeat as necessary.

Too salty – Add a little sugar and vinegar. For soups or sauces, add a raw peeled potato.

Too sweet – Add a little vinegar or lemon juice.

Undercooked cakes and cookies – Serve over vanilla ice cream. You can also layer pieces of cake or cookies with whipped cream and fresh fruit to form a dessert parfait. Crumbled cookies also make an excellent ice cream or cream pie topping.

COUNTING CALORIES

BEVERAGES

apple juice, 6 oz. 90
coffee (black) 0
cola, 12 oz. 115
cranberry juice, 6 oz. 115
ginger ale, 12 oz. 115
grape juice, (prepared from
    frozen concentrate), 6 oz. 142
lemonade, (prepared from
    frozen concentrate), 6 oz. 85
milk, protein fortified, 1 c. 105
    skim, 1 c. 90
    whole, 1 c. 160
orange juice, 6 oz. 85
pineapple juice, unsweetened, 6 oz. 95
root beer, 12 oz. 150
tonic (quinine water) 12 oz. 132

BREADS

cornbread, 1 sm. square 130
dumplings, 1 med. 70
French toast, 1 slice........................135
melba toast, 1 slice 25
muffins, blueberry, 1 muffin 110
    bran, 1 muffin.............................106
    corn, 1 muffin 125
    English, 1 muffin 280
pancakes, 1 (4-in.) 60
pumpernickel, 1 slice 75
rye, 1 slice 60
waffle, 1 216
white, 1 slice 60-70
whole wheat, 1 slice 55-65

CEREALS

cornflakes, 1 c. 105
cream of wheat, 1 c. 120
oatmeal, 1 c. 148
rice flakes, 1 c. 105
shredded wheat, 1 biscuit 100
sugar krisps, 3/4 c. 110

CRACKERS

graham, 1 cracker 15-30
rye crisp, 1 cracker............................35
saltine, 1 cracker...........................17-20
wheat thins, 1 cracker 9

DAIRY PRODUCTS

butter or margarine, 1 T. 100
cheese, American, 1 oz. 100
    camembert, 1 oz. 85
    cheddar, 1 oz. 115
    cottage cheese, 1 oz. 30
    mozzarella, 1 oz. 90
    parmesan, 1 oz. 130
    ricotta, 1 oz. 50
    roquefort, 1 oz. 105
    Swiss, 1 oz. 105
cream, light, 1 T. 30
    heavy, 1 T. 55
    sour, 1 T. 45
hot chocolate, with milk, 1 c. 277
milk chocolate, 1 oz. 145-155
yogurt
    made w/ whole milk, 1 c. 150-165
    made w/ skimmed milk, 1 c. 125

EGGS

fried, 1 lg. 100
poached or boiled, 1 lg. 75-80
scrambled or in omelet, 1 lg. 110-130

FISH AND SEAFOOD

bass, 4 oz. 105
salmon, broiled or baked, 3 oz. 155
sardines, canned in oil, 3 oz. 170
trout, fried, 3 1/2 oz. 220
tuna, in oil, 3 oz. 170
    in water, 3 oz. 110

COUNTING CALORIES

FRUITS

apple, 1 med. 80-100
applesauce, sweetened, 1/2 c. 90-115
   unsweetened, 1/2 c. 50
banana, 1 med. 85
blueberries, 1/2 c. 45
cantaloupe, 1/2 c. 24
cherries (pitted), raw, 1/2 c. 40
grapefruit, 1/2 med. 55
grapes, 1/2 c. 35-55
honeydew, 1/2 c. 55
mango, 1 med. 90
orange, 1 med. 65-75
peach, 1 med. 35
pear, 1 med. 60-100
pineapple, fresh, 1/2 c. 40
   canned in syrup, 1/2 c. 95
plum, 1 med. 30
strawberries, fresh, 1/2 c. 30
   frozen and sweetened, 1/2 c. ..120-140
tangerine, 1 lg. 39
watermelon, 1/2 c. 42

MEAT AND POULTRY

beef, ground (lean), 3 oz. 185
   roast, 3 oz. 185
chicken, broiled, 3 oz. 115
lamb chop (lean), 3 oz. 175-200
steak, sirloin, 3 oz. 175
   tenderloin, 3 oz. 174
   top round, 3 oz. 162
turkey, dark meat, 3 oz. 175
   white meat, 3 oz. 150
veal, cutlet, 3 oz. 156
   roast, 3 oz. 76

NUTS

almonds, 2 T. 105
cashews, 2 T. 100
peanuts, 2 T. 105
peanut butter, 1 T. 95
pecans, 2 T. 95
pistachios, 2 T. 92
walnuts, 2 T. 80

PASTA

macaroni or spaghetti,
   cooked, 3/4 c. 115

SALAD DRESSINGS

blue cheese, 1 T. 70
French, 1 T. 65
Italian, 1 T. 80
mayonnaise, 1 T. 100
olive oil, 1 T. 124
Russian, 1 T. 70
salad oil, 1 T. 120

SOUPS

bean, 1 c. 130-180
beef noodle, 1 c. 70
bouillon and consomme, 1 c. 30
chicken noodle, 1 c. 65
chicken with rice, 1 c. 50
minestrone, 1 c. 80-150
split pea, 1 c. 145-170
tomato with milk, 1 c. 170
vegetable, 1 c. 80-100

VEGETABLES

asparagus, 1 c. 35
broccoli, cooked, 1/2 c. 25
cabbage, cooked, 1/2 c. 15-20
carrots, cooked, 1/2 c. 25-30
cauliflower, 1/2 c. 10-15
corn (kernels), 1/2 c. 70
green beans, 1 c. 30
lettuce, shredded, 1/2 c. 5
mushrooms, canned, 1/2 c. 20
onions, cooked, 1/2 c. 30
peas, cooked, 1/2 c. 60
potato, baked, 1 med. 90
   chips, 8-10 100
   mashed, w/milk & butter, 1 c. ..200-300
spinach, 1 c. 40
tomato, raw, 1 med. 25
   cooked, 1/2 c. 30

COOKING TERMS

Au gratin: Topped with crumbs and/or cheese and browned in oven or under broiler.

Au jus: Served in its own juices.

Baste: To moisten foods during cooking with pan drippings or special sauce in order to add flavor and prevent drying.

Bisque: A thick cream soup.

Blanch: To immerse in rapidly boiling water and allow to cook slightly.

Cream: To soften a fat, especially butter, by beating it at room temperature. Butter and sugar are often creamed together, making a smooth, soft paste.

Crimp: To seal the edges of a two-crust pie either by pinching them at intervals with the fingers or by pressing them together with the tines of a fork.

Crudites: An assortment of raw vegetables (i.e. carrots, broccoli, celery, mushrooms) that is served as an hors d'oeuvre, often accompanied by a dip.

Degrease: To remove fat from the surface of stews, soups or stock. Usually cooled in the refrigerator so that fat hardens and is easily removed.

Dredge: To coat lightly with flour, cornmeal, etc.

Entree: The main course.

Fold: To incorporate a delicate substance, such as whipped cream or beaten egg whites, into another substance without releasing air bubbles. A spatula is used to gently bring part of the mixture from the bottom of the bowl to the top. The process is repeated, while slowly rotating the bowl, until the ingredients are thoroughly blended.

Glaze: To cover with a glossy coating, such as a melted and somewhat diluted jelly for fruit desserts.

Julienne: To cut or slice vegetables, fruits or cheeses into match-shaped slivers.

Marinate: To allow food to stand in a liquid in order to tenderize or to add flavor.

Meuniére: Dredged with flour and sautéed in butter.

Mince: To chop food into very small pieces.

Parboil: To boil until partially cooked; to blanch. Usually final cooking in a seasoned sauce follows this procedure.

Pare: To remove the outermost skin of a fruit or vegetable.

Poach: To cook gently in hot liquid kept just below the boiling point.

Purée: To mash foods by hand by rubbing through a sieve or food mill, or by whirling in a blender or food processor until perfectly smooth.

Refresh: To run cold water over food that has been parboiled in order to stop the cooking process quickly.

Sauté: To cook and/or brown food in a small quantity of hot shortening.

Scald: To heat to just below the boiling point, when tiny bubbles appear at the edge of the saucepan.

Simmer: To cook in liquid just below the boiling point. The surface of the liquid should be barely moving, broken from time to time by slowly rising bubbles.

Steep: To let food stand in hot liquid in order to extract or to enhance flavor, like tea in hot water or poached fruit in syrup.

Toss: To combine ingredients with a repeated lifting motion.

Whip: To beat rapidly in order to incorporate air and produce expansion, as in heavy cream or egg whites.

Morris Press Cookbooks has all the right ingredients to make a really great cookbook. Your group can raise $500–$50,000 or create a cookbook as a lasting keepsake, preserving favorite family recipes.

3 ways to order our **FREE** Cookbook Kit:

- Call us at **800-445-6621, ext. CB**.
- Visit our web site at **www.morriscookbooks.com**.
- Complete and mail the **postage-paid reply card** below.